# STAINED GLASS PATCHWORK

## CONTENTS

## GAIL LAWTHER

TEAMWORK
CRAFTBOOKS

# Introduction & Materials

**WELCOME TO STAINED GLASS PATCHWORK.** *Over the past few years I've done many talks and workshops on this very dramatic (and also very easy!) method, and I've seen a growing interest in it among quilters. During this time I've often been asked if there is a book devoted specifically to stained glass patchwork. As far as I know, this is the first! I've wanted to write it for years, and now that wish has become reality: I hope you enjoy reading and working with the book as much as I've enjoyed putting it together.*

## What is Stained Glass Patchwork?

As you can see from the examples on the cover, this technique gets its name from its similarity to stained glass windows. And the way that stained glass quilts are put together is very like the way a stained glass window is assembled. With the window the pieces of glass are cut to shape and then put together like a jigsaw, with the joins between shapes filled with leading: with the patchwork, pieces of fabric are cut to shape and the joins between shapes are covered with lines of tape or bias binding. So really, despite its name, the technique is actually a method of appliqué, rather than seamed patchwork.

## Is it suitable for beginners?

If you're completely new to quilting, you couldn't choose a simpler method for producing quick and striking results. Because of the way the designs are produced there are no tricky seams – in fact, no patchwork seams at all – and you don't even need to be too accurate when you're cutting out the fabric pieces, because small errors will be covered by the lines of bias binding or tape. The technique lends itself to bold, quite large designs, so the fabric patches are usually quite large and therefore the work grows quickly.

It's perfectly possible for even a complete beginner to complete an easy project, such as the mirror, the cream and gold cushion cover or the teacosy, in a couple of hours.

If you have done some quilting, but not all that much, once again you will find this a very simple technique to master. Try things like the sofa throw, the ammonite mat, or the Bethlehem scene. Some of the tips and ideas may spark off your own ideas for using or developing the basic technique.

If you are already an accomplished quilter, you will find it easy to do the more complicated projects such as the holly banner, the rose wall-hangings, the lotus floor-cushion and the waves bed quilt. These are all put together in exactly the same way as the smaller projects: they are just much larger items, or have more complicated stitching sequences.

Generally, the projects in the book begin with the very easiest, using straight lines with no junctions. The projects then move into curved lines, for instance on the teacosy, but still with no junctions. Gradually through the book they get increasingly more challenging, moving right up to a double bed quilt as the grand finale.

## Do I need any special equipment?

No – nothing that you haven't already got in your sewing box or pencil-case. Stained glass patchwork probably uses even less equipment than most other patchwork techniques, as there is very little measuring and no complicated shape-cutting. These basic items will be all you need for most projects – anything extra, such as the occasional reel of quilting thread or tube of glue, will be specified under the Materials list for each project.

- pins
- tacking and general sewing thread: you can use either a cotton thread, such as Sylko, or a synthetic thread such as Drima
- embroidery scissors (small, sharp scissors)

- cutting-out scissors
- needles in several sizes, for tacking and hand-sewing
- thimble if you usually use one
- tape measure
- unpicker (well, we all make mistakes …!)
- ruler (because some of the patterns are quite large, you may find a long quilter's rule or a yardstick useful)
- soft pencil
- paper for enlarging patterns
- black felt pen
- paper scissors (don't use your fabric scissors for paper, as it blunts them quickly)

## Should I stitch by hand or machine?

One of the great advantages of stained glass patchwork is that every stage can be stitched by machine if you wish, making it extra-quick. All of the projects within this book were stitched by machine. If you prefer hand-sewing, though, there is no reason at all why you shouldn't use it: every project can be stitched by hand, it just takes a bit longer. Hand-stitching does mean, though, that you can take a piece on holiday with you and sit and stitch when you wouldn't want to be using a machine.

## Do I need any special materials?

Once again, the answer is no. Any fabric that is suitable for other sewing projects is suitable for stained glass patchwork. Some people prefer to use all cotton fabrics, the traditional choice of the quilter: I've used these in many of the projects, but when an item doesn't need to be washable I like to use unusual fabrics, such as the shiny fabrics in the blue mirror and the flower wall-hangings, and the metallic fabrics you can see in the Bethlehem scenes. Some furnishing fabrics can also be very effective.

If you are making an item and want to be able to launder it, the usual rules for preparing your fabric apply. Wash it first in warm-to-hot soapy water, to pre-shrink it and make sure that it is colour-fast. If the colour does run, keep rinsing it in cold water; if it's still 'bleeding', it's best to discard it and choose another as the colour will

continue to run during washing. Press all fabrics before you mark or cut them, so that you can be sure you are cutting accurate patches.

When you're doing conventional patchwork, it's usually important to cut the patches along the grain – the weave – of the fabric. This ensures that the seams don't distort when the patches are joined. In stained glass patchwork the grain of the fabric is not really important, as the patches aren't going to be seamed.

## Are the projects quilted?

I've done the projects in the book as a mixture of quilted and flat designs: for instance, the Bethlehem scene is flat, and so is the lotus cushion-cover, while the iris wall-hanging is quilted and so is the waves bed quilt. This is almost entirely a matter of personal preference, though: if you want to make the rose wall-hangings so that they are quilted rather than flat, there's nothing at all to stop you – just add wadding at the relevant point, quilt the project by hand or machine, and bind it or back it in an appropriate way.

The wadding you choose for a project will depend on the final effect you are aiming for. Polyester wadding is synthetic and washable, and comes in several different thicknesses; the one used most commonly by quilters is 2oz, which I used in the bed quilt and the holly banner, but I've used 4oz in the pinboard so that there is a thicker padded layer. For the iris wall-hanging I wanted a more subtle padding, so I used a layer of dolmette, a heavier, more compact wadding.

## How do I use the Pattern Library?

I've included ten pages packed with extra designs in the centre of the book; this is the Pattern Library, and you can use these drawings as starting points for creating your own stained glass patchwork projects. Some of the designs are simple and some are complicated; all of them can be enlarged to any size you wish and adapted for all kinds of different items: so, for instance, a square pattern could be used at any size from a herb cushion to a double bed quilt. Try out unsual fabrics, and different colour schemes for fabric and binding. Have fun experimenting!

# The Basic Technique

## Choosing your binding

All the designs used in the project have some kind of binding that's used to cover the joins between the fabric patches. This binding serves several purposes: it conceals the raw edges, it also secures them under a line of stitching and so prevents them from fraying, and it also plays a large part in the appearance of the finished design. It's because of this final point that you generally use a colour or shade of binding that contrasts with your fabric patches – so that the lines of binding stand out instead of disappearing into the background.

The type of binding you use will depend on the nature of the project. For lines that curve you will need bias binding. This is cut diagonally across the grain of the fabric so that it has some stretch; the stretch allows you to ease it round curved lines, which makes it perfect for stained glass patchwork. Where the lines of the design are straight, for instance for the first couple of projects in this book, you don't need to have any stretch, so you can use any straight ribbon, binding, seam binding or coloured tape.

You can buy bias binding in many different colours, several different widths, and at least two types of fabric: the most common fabric is cotton, but you can also use satin bias binding which has a lovely sheen. Wider bias binding is used for larger projects (such as the bed quilt), for more dramatic outlines (such as the border of the clown nursery hanging), and when you want actually to bind one part of the project as well as using it between the patches (for example on the teacosy). Coats do a good range of coordinating cotton bias bindings in different widths.

You don't have to use binding in a single colour, of course: patterned ribbons (for straight lines) and bias bindings (for curves) are available, and you can also cut your own from fabric. The simple tools available for folding home-made bias-binding accurately can be quite useful.

## Building up the design

The most important thing about stained glass patchwork is the order in which you apply the lines of binding. For the first few projects of the book, I've designed the patterns so that the lines of binding don't have any junctions: they may be parallel, as with the mirror, or cross each other, as with the teacosy and the cream-and-gold cushion, but all the lines of binding can be added and stitched at the same stage.

On more complicated designs, such as the peacock feather curtain and the holly banner, the order in which the strips are added is an important part of creating the pattern. In these, there are parts of the design where one line of binding goes into another in what I call a T-junction. At the T-junctions, you have to lay the first line of binding (the stem of the T) first, so that the next line of binding (the cross-bar of the T) will conceal its raw end. The examples 1-5, opposite, show how this works in practice on a 'Broken Heart' design.

## Finishing tips

Very occasionally, you will need to finish off the raw end of a piece of binding without being able to tuck it under a subsequent line. When this happens, fold the raw end under itself and stitch it into place as usual. When an end is tapered to a point, fold it under in a long diagonal to produce the taper.

Bias binding will hold its stretch even better if you press each curve with a steam iron to set it before you stitch it. Where curves are very tight, pleat them evenly or run a gathering thread round the inside curve to ease it. At corners and points, pleat or fold the binding crisply. When you are stitching a curved line, where possible stitch along the inside edge of the curve first: if you stitch the outside first it can stretch the binding too much. Stitch either by hand, or by machine using a narrow zigzag stitch.

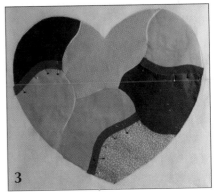

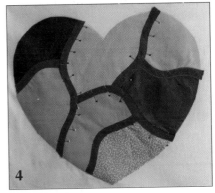

Like many other professional stitchers, I use a Bernina sewing machine; the photograph shows me trying out one of Bernina's new 170 models. I'm sitting in front of my very first stained glass quilt – which still looks dramatic after quite a few years!

1 *The basic lines of the design traced onto the backing fabric.*
2 *All the fabric patches have been cut to shape and put in position on the traced background – like assembling the pieces of a jigsaw puzzle.*
3 *The first lines going into T-junctions are pinned in place, and have been steam pressed to set the curves. They will now be stitched down each side by hand or machine.*
4 *The other lines of the design are added in the same way.*
5 *The finished design, outlined by a final length of binding.*

# How to Use the Charts

## Enlarging

Apart from the pinboard, each project in this book has a chart, or trace-off, giving you the basic lines of the design. The first thing to do is to enlarge the design to the correct size; this will be given alongside the chart.

You can enlarge the design in one of two ways. When the enlargement is not too enormous, for instance the ammonite mat, you may be able to do it on a photocopier. Generally, though, you will need to copy it larger – either using the grid method, or drawing by eye if you are confident!

## Using the keys

Some designs have a key alongside the chart: this simply shows you which fabric goes where, just like using a paint-by-numbers design. On these charts you will sometimes find sections that are blank: blank areas indicate that no extra fabric patch is cut for that section, so that the background fabric shows. On some designs there is no need for a key as the fabrics are not specified exactly; you decide which fabric looks best in which position!

## Following the stitching sequence

Along with each chart goes a stitching sequence, which tells you the order in which to build up the lines of binding. The stitching sequence for each design makes sure that all the raw ends of bias binding are sealed under subsequent lines. When the designs are quite complex, the stitching sequences look quite complicated too, but as you begin to follow each one you will see that they are actually very logical.

The series of charts here shows how one of the Bethlehem scenes (shown on page 48) is built up, following the different stages of its stitching sequence. The fine lines show how the basic design looks after all the fabrics have been put into place; the heavy lines show the lines of bias binding being built up in sequence.

## STITCHING SEQUENCE:

A Begin with the castle wall at the top of the design, the two pointed doorways (9 and 10), the top two steps of the staircase, the pointed dome at the top of the tower (5), and the small dome near the bottom of the design (12).
*(These lines are done first either because they stand independently, such as the two doors, or because they come into T-junctions with other lines of the design)*

B Now add the large dome (3) under the castle wall, and the top and left-hand edge of the small building at the centre bottom (13).
*(The first line seals the inner end of the castle wall binding: the second line seals both ends of the small dome above it)*

C Next, bind the top and tiny right-hand edge of the large central building (4).
*(This line seals the ends of the binding round the large dome)*

D Now you can do the smaller dome (7) to the right of the design.
*(The line around this dome seals the end of the binding around building 4)*

E Finish off the building on the right (8) by covering its top and left-hand edge. Use one long line of binding to cover the top and right-hand edge of the tower (6), and take the same strip down the remaining parts of the staircase to outline piece 10.
*(The first of these lines seals the binding round dome 7: the long line then seals all the raw ends it covers)*

F Finally, do the window-frames (14 and 15) in the centre of the design.
*(These shapes stand on their own. The line of binding round each one seals the raw edges of the fabric, and the raw ends of the binding are tucked under themselves and stitched in place)*

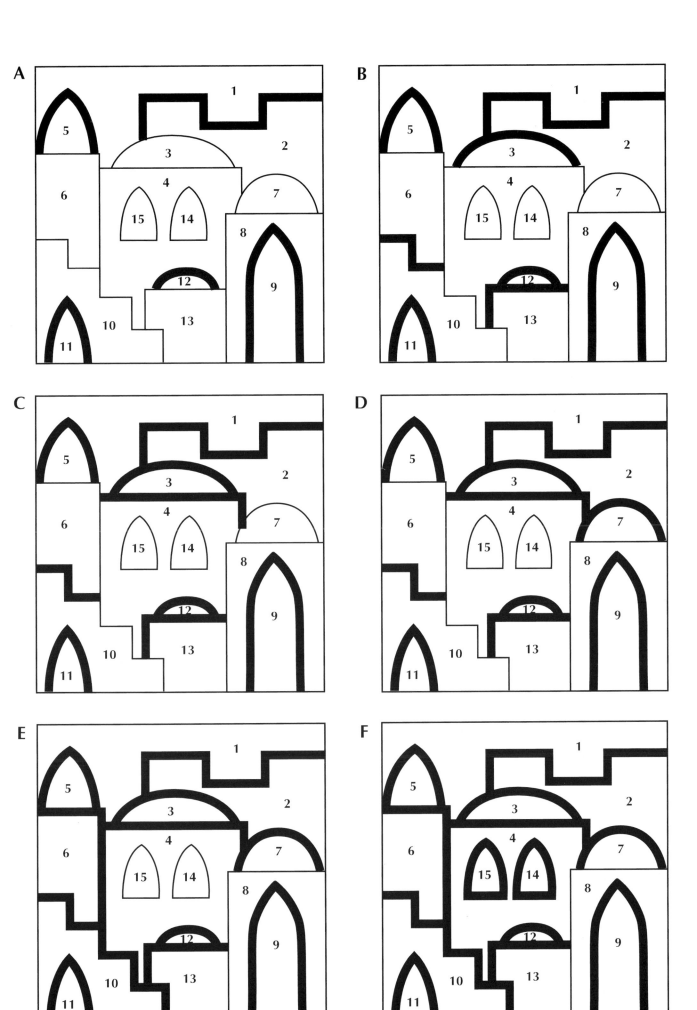

# PROJECT 1

# Stripy Mirror Frame

*These dramatic mirror frames show stained glass patchwork at its simplest: all the lines of the design are straight, and are covered with ribbon, tape or seam binding.*

*The two very different examples show how changing the colour-scheme alters the whole appearance of the design. The top frame is worked in mid-tones of rainbow colours, edged with white braid, and would work very well in a nursery or a child's room. The second version uses exotic fabrics in tones of pink, blue and purple, and would look good anywhere!*

## PREPARATION

1  Enlarge the pattern on page 10 to the correct size, and go over the lines with black felt pen to make them stronger. Write in the numbers of the pieces; these will help you identify which bit you are dealing with when you cut out the templates.

2  Press all the coloured fabrics and the backing pieces. Lay one of the backing pieces over the enlarged design and trace the design onto it in pencil or crayon.

## MAKING UP THE BLUE MIRROR

3  Decide which fabric you will use for each piece; the best way to do this is simply to put each piece of fabric down on a table and try others next to it until you feel that you have found the most effective arrangement. Try to mix up the different colours and tones across the design. Once you have decided on your fabric sequence, cut your drawn design into sections and use each piece as a template to cut the correct shape from the relevant fabric. You may find it less confusing to cut and position one piece at a time, working your way across the square, instead of cutting all the templates out together.

4  Put the pieces, right sides up, like a jigsaw puzzle over the traced design on your square, and check that you are happy with the way the different fabrics work together. If you are unhappy with any piece, re-cut it using a different piece of fabric. Once all the fabrics are in position, tack them carefully with small stitches: slippery

## MATERIALS FOR THE BLUE MIRROR FRAME

- Two 14in (36cm) squares of navy blue backing fabric
- Scraps of six different fabrics in blues, purples and pinks
- 2yd/2m of navy blue satin or velvet ribbon
- Navy blue Drima or Sylko sewing thread
- Four beads in a toning colour
- Two 12in (30cm) squares of firm cardboard
- Mirror tile 6in (15cm) square
- Short length of navy blue cord
- Pale crayon, special marker for dark fabrics, or dressmakers' carbon paper in a light colour
- Paper, pencil, black felt pen etc for enlarging the pattern
- Glue and masking tape

## MATERIALS FOR THE RAINBOW MIRROR FRAME

- Two 14in (36cm) squares of white backing fabric
- Scraps of six different fabrics in rainbow colours
- 2yd/2m of white braid
- White Drima or Sylko sewing thread
- Four white beads
- Two 12in (30cm) squares of firm cardboard
- Mirror tile 6in (15cm) square
- Short length of white cord
- Soft pencil
- Paper, pencil, black felt pen etc for enlarging the pattern
- Glue and masking tape

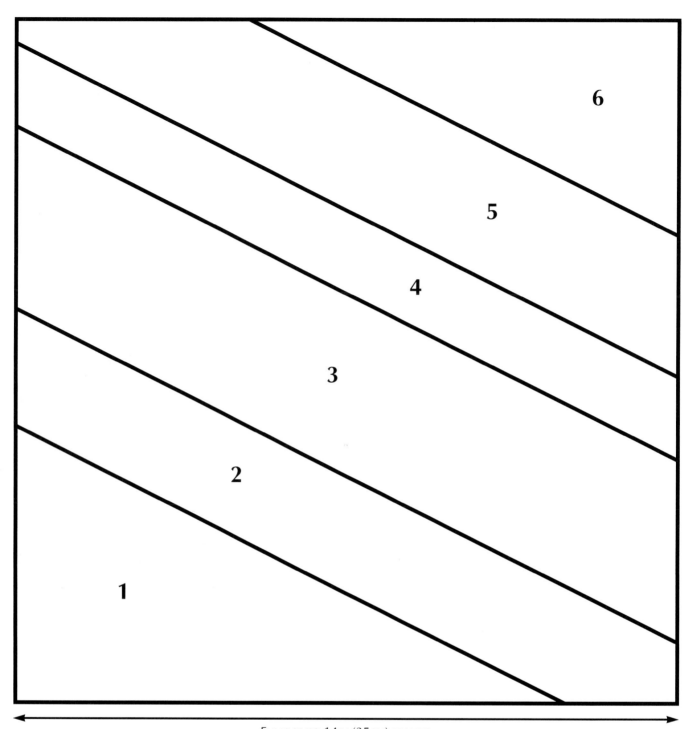

ENLARGE TO 14IN (35CM) SQUARE

## STITCHING SEQUENCE:

*All the lines of this design are added
and secured at the same stage.*

fabrics like this tend to distort and move out of position very easily, so it's worth taking the time to anchor them securely.

5   Cut a strip of ribbon to go across each line of the design. Squeeze a line of glue down the centre back of each ribbon strip and leave for a few minutes until the glue is almost dry – this means that it is less likely to smear the fabrics as you position it. Carefully lay each strip in position and press it into place.

## Finishing

6   While you wait for the glue to dry completely, mark a 5in (13cm) square in the exact centre of one piece of card. Lay the square of decorated fabric, right side up, over the front of this card mount and fold the raw edges over to the back, mitring the corners neatly. Glue the excess fabric to the back of the mount, or stick it down with masking tape.

7   Using sharp scissors, carefully cut a square of fabric away from the centre of the frame, cutting $3/4$in (2cm) inside the edge of the card. Snip into the corners to within $1/8$in (2mm) of the corner of the mount; don't cut any closer, or the fabric will start to fray at the corners. Fold these edges to the back and secure them.

8   Using toning thread, stitch a bead into each corner. This seals the corners neatly, and means that you can't see bare card reflected in the mirror when it's finished.

9   Lay the second piece of backing fabric, right side up, over the second square of card; fold the raw edges to the back and stick them in position with glue or masking tape.

10  Lay this square of card, fabric side down, on a flat surface and use glue or adhesive tabs to stick the mirror tile into the exact centre of the card. Don't use masking tape for this stage, as the inner edges of the tape may show when the frame is complete.

11  Put the two pieces of card together, fabric sides out. Using a large, sharp needle, stitch them together round the edges with oversewing. When you come to the corner for the hanging loop, cut a 5in (13cm) length of cord, form it into a loop, and slip the raw ends between the pieces of card: stitch the loop into place firmly, then continue stitching round the edges. If you prefer, you can edge the entire mirror frame with cord: if you want to stitch it round the inner edge of the frame, it's easier to do that part before you stitch the two panels together.

## Rainbow Variation

At stages 3 and 4, cut and position the fabrics so that they follow the colours of a rainbow – it doesn't matter which colour you begin with, as long as they follow in the correct sequence! At stage 5, work in the same way but with strips of white braid in place of the ribbon; the rest of the assembly is the same as for the blue frame.

## Handy Hints

*Try using a curved needle, like the ones used by upholsterers, for stitching the two sections of the frame together. The curve means that the needle naturally comes up away from the fabric each time you take a stitch, making it easier to grasp ready for the next stitch.*

*DIY stores sell mirror tiles in different sizes; the tiles often come with their own adhesive tabs, which are ideal for securing them to the frame backing.*

*To make positioning the mirror tile easy, draw the diagonals on the second square of card. Put the mirror so that one corner is on each diagonal – then you'll know the mirror is in the centre.*

# PROJECT 2

# Cream and Gold Cushion

*The combination of cream and gold always looks wonderful, and this cushion cover makes full use of the unusual patterned and textured fabrics available in those colours today. Because the lines of the design aren't curved, you don't need bias binding: the lines here are made with strips of gold lamé fabric, but you could use a toning ribbon, or golden satin fabric.*

## MATERIALS

- One piece of cream calico or sheeting, 16in (41cm) square
- Large scraps of five or six different cream-and-gold, or plain cream, fabrics; try to find unusual fabrics, to add to the visual interest
- Two pieces of firm cream backing fabric, such as thick calico, each 16 x 12in (41 x 30cm)
- 4yd (4m) strips of gold fabric, 1¹/₄in (3cm) wide unfolded (or the same amount of gold ribbon, ¹/₂in (12mm) wide)
- Cream Sylko or Drima sewing thread
- Metallic gold thread suitable for machine stitching
- Yellow or brown pencil
- Paper, pencil, black felt pen etc for enlarging the pattern
- 15in (38cm) square cushion pad

## PREPARATION

1 Enlarge the pattern on page 15 to the correct size, and go over all the lines with a black felt pen to make them darker.

2 Press the calico or sheeting and lay it on top of the enlarged design; using a yellow or brown pencil, trace the lines of the design onto the fabric.

## MAKING UP

3 Press all the cream and gold fabrics and decide which fabric you are going to use for each section of the design. Scatter them well across the design, and make sure that no two adjoining pieces are in the same fabric. Once you have decided, cut out the different sections of the design, one at a time, and use the pieces as templates to cut shapes from the appropriate fabrics.

4 Lay the pieces on the marked fabric right sides up, like a jigsaw puzzle, and check that you are happy with the way the different fabrics work together. If you are unhappy with any piece, re-cut it using a new piece of fabric. Tack the pieces in position, or pin them firmly if you prefer.

5 If you are using fabric to make your binding, press the raw edges to the back to make a strip half an inch (12mm) wide. (Omit this stage if you are using ribbon.)

6 Cut strips of your binding to fit the lines of the design, and lay them in position across the cushion design: the order of the strips doesn't matter, as all the raw ends will be sealed in the edge seam of the cushion cover. Don't add strips of binding round the outside edges of the design – only along the lines that go across the square. Tack or pin the strips in place.

**7** Stitch the strips down each side by hand or machine. If you are stitching by machine, simply stitch straight across the junctions when the strips cross. If you are using metallic fabric, you may find that strands of the fabric get caught up and pulled out of place by the needle: if this happens, try putting a ball-point needle in your machine for this part of the stitching.

## FINISHING

**8** When all the strips have been stitched into place, lay the whole design face down and press it from the back. Check that the fabric is still in an even square; if not, trim the edges to straighten it up.

**9** Fold over and stitch a small double hem along one long edge of each piece of backing fabric. Lay the stained glass design on a flat surface, right side up, and position the two backing pieces on top, right sides down, and with their raw edges level with the fabric square so that they overlap. Pin and tack a half inch (12mm) seam all the way around the edges of the square.

**10** Stitch the seam by machine: at the corners and when you stitch over the hems of the backing pieces, go over the stitching line two or three times to strengthen it. Clip the corners diagonally and trim the seams to within $1/4$in (5mm) of the stitching line.

**11** Turn the cushion-cover right side out and push out the corners: press. Insert the cushion pad.

## QUILTED VARIATIONS

If you'd like to quilt your cushion cover, there are various easy ways that you can do it.

- If you prefer to quilt by machine, you can do the quilting at the same time as stitching on your gold strips. Follow the main instructions up to stage 6, then cut 16in (41cm) squares of muslin and 2oz wadding. Lay the muslin on a flat surface and cover with the wadding: add the stained glass piece, right side up, and tack the three layers together with a grid of horizontal and vertical lines of tacking. Stitch the lines of binding on as usual, and your work will be quilted simultaneously.

- If you prefer to quilt by hand, follow the main instructions up to stage 7. Then cut the squares of muslin and wadding and make a quilt 'sandwich' with them as described above. Using gold thread in short lengths, or cream quilting thread, quilt each patch with running stitch about $1/4$in (5mm) inside the line of gold binding.

For either technique, make up the cushion cover in the same way as described in the main instructions, but remember that you can't iron quilted items as you will flatten the wadding. After you have stitched the outer seam and turned the cover out, press it just at the very edges to set the seam without squashing the wadding.

ENLARGE TO 16IN (41CM) SQUARE

## VARIATIONS

*This bold design works well in any colour-scheme; pick out colours and tones to suit your own decor. Choose four or five different fabrics that complement each other, then select a dark or light binding in a colour that shows them all off well.*

**STITCHING SEQUENCE:**

*All the lines of this design are added and stitched at the same stage.*

# PROJECT 3

# Lattice Pinboard

*OK, so this one's a shameless cheat! On this cheerful pinboard, the stained glass effect is created by using a checked fabric and covering the lines of the check design with ribbon. The ribbon strips are only secured on the back, so that they make a lattice shape across the front of the board. You can use the lattice to hold notes, photographs, birthday reminders, appointment cards, postcards etc – you know, all those little scraps of paper with addresses and phone numbers on them that always go missing …*

## PREPARATION

1  Press the checked fabric, and place the backing board on it diagonally so that there is a margin round each edge and the checked design is at exactly 45° to the edges of the board. If you mark the halfway points along each edge of the board, that will help you to make sure that the fabric design is positioned evenly. Cut a fabric piece 3in (7.5cm) larger all round than the board.

2  Put a few dabs of glue on the front of the backing board and allow it to dry slightly; then position the piece of wadding on top. Leave this to dry completely: if you start to make up the board while the glue is still wet it may come through the wadding and mark the checked fabric.

## MAKING UP

3  Lay the board, wadding side down, on the wrong side of the fabric piece and begin folding the edges over. Fold each edge over in a double hem so that it looks neat. Begin with one of the long edges; as you fold each edge, hold it in position with pieces of masking tape while you fold the others. You want the fabric firmly pulled over the wadding, but not stretched so taut that the wadding is flattened. Every so often, turn the board over so that you can check that the pattern is still straight. Fold the corners neatly, either straight or in mitres.

4  Beginning at one corner, lay strips of ribbon over the main lines of the fabric pattern; secure each end of each strip at the back of the board with an upholstery pin. Remove the masking tape in each section as you pin it. If the pins are difficult to push in, use a hammer for extra help! Your board is now ready for use.

## MATERIALS

- Firm wood or pinboard to use as a backing – this one began life as a cheap pinboard measuring 16 x 24in (40 x 60cm)
- Piece of 4oz wadding the same size as your backing board
- about 1yd/1m of firm cotton fabric with a large, regular checked design
- Two packs of upholstery pins or large tacks
- 9yd/9m satin ribbon, $5/8$in (15mm) wide – I used two shades of green, but you'll need to choose colours that tone with your fabric
- Masking tape

## STITCHING SEQUENCE:

A  *Begin working from one top corner diagonally across the board.*

B  *Then add the other ribbon strips at right angles to the first lines, working from the other top corner downwards.*

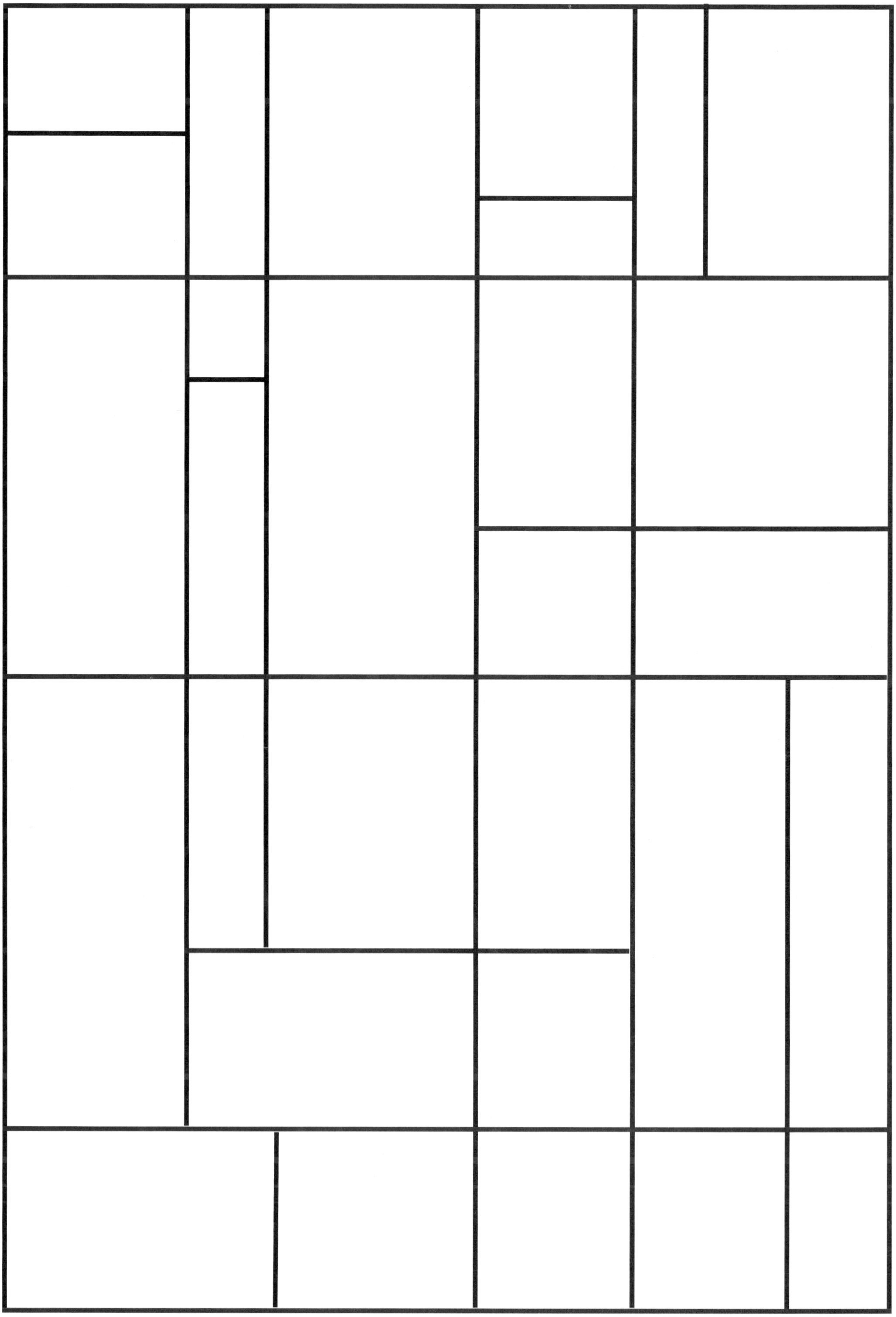

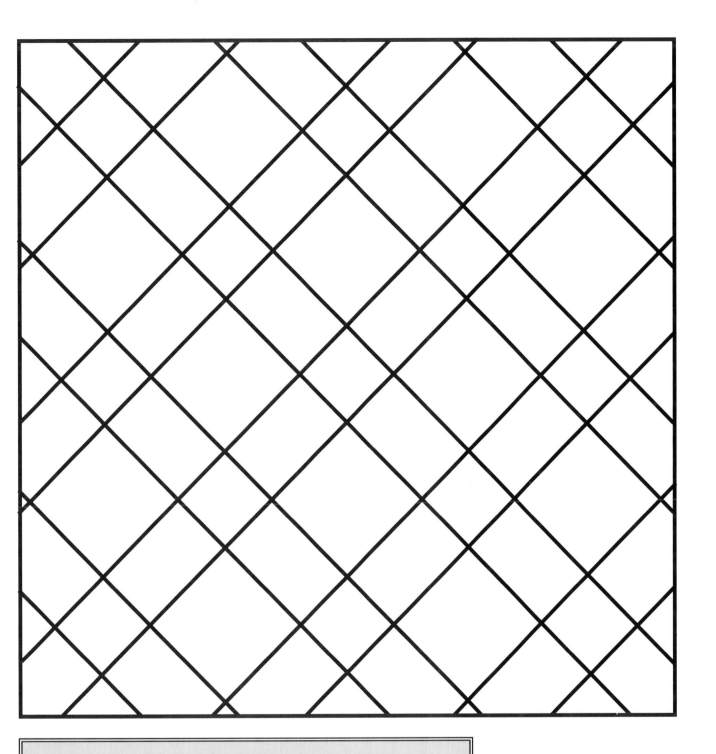

## VARIATIONS

*These pages show two totally different ways of creating your pinboard. With a plain fabric backing you could try a more elaborate lattice design such as the one above, perhaps using three or four colours of ribbon.*

*Or, for a stylish office, try the Mondrian-style design opposite; use black ribbon over patches of plain fabric in primary colours and white, and secure the lines that go part-way across first with small tacks.*

# Classy Teacosy

## MATERIALS

- Large scraps of five or six different toning fabrics, plains and prints
- Three pieces of plain cotton fabric in a toning colour, 16 x 12in (41 x 30cm)
- One extra piece of one of your print fabrics, for the back of the teacosy, 16 x 12in (41 x 30cm)
- Two pieces of 2oz or 4oz wadding, 16 x 12in (41 x 30cm)
- 3yd/3m Coats cotton bias binding in a toning colour, $^1$/2in (12mm) wide when folded
- 2$^1$/2yd/2.5m Coats cotton bias binding in the same colour, 1in (2.5cm) wide when folded
- Matching Sylko or Drima sewing thread
- Soft pencil
- Paper, pencil, black felt pen etc for enlarging the pattern

---

### VARIATIONS

*Pick out fabrics to match your tea-service for this design, or use oddments of fabric left over from dining-room curtains; then choose a darker bias binding to contrast.*

---

*Now we're going into curves, using bias binding instead of tape or ribbon. This simple teacosy design provides an easy introduction for your first use of curved lines between the fabric patches. You don't even need to worry about a stitching sequence, as all the raw ends of the bias binding are concealed in the extra line of wider binding that goes across the bottom and round the curved edge of the teacosy.*

## PREPARATION

1 Enlarge the pattern on pages 22-23 to the correct size, and go over the lines with a felt pen to make them darker. Write the numbers in faintly, in case they show through any of the paler patches.

2 Lay one of the pieces of foundation fabric over the enlarged design and trace the lines in pencil. Following the traced outline of your design, cut this piece of fabric to the teacosy shape, then cut the other foundation pieces, the backing section and the two pieces of wadding to the same shape.

## MAKING UP

3 Decide which fabric you are putting where, then cut the enlarged pattern along the marked lines, section by section, and use these pieces as templates to cut patches out of the appropriate fabrics. Put all the pieces inside the marked design on the foundation piece, right side up, assembling them like a jigsaw puzzle; tack them into place.

4 Cut six strips of the narrow binding to fit the lines of the design, and tack them in position across the teacosy: the order of the strips doesn't matter, as all the raw ends will be sealed in eventually. Stitch down both sides of the binding curves by hand or machine.

## FINISHING

5 Put one of the spare foundation pieces on a flat surface, right side down, and smooth out any wrinkles; cover this with a layer of wadding, and then the stained glass piece, right side up. Pin the three layers together to stop them from moving around while you stitch, then cut a strip of the wider binding the same length as the straight bottom edge of the shape. Unfold one of the edges of the

binding and tack it along the straight edge, matching the raw edges. Stitch the seam, then fold the binding over to the lining side and slipstitch the other edge in place. Make up the back of the teacosy in the same way, using the spare piece of printed fabric on the outside.

6   Put the front and back sections of the teacosy together, right sides out, and tack through all the layers. Use the wider bias binding to bind in a smooth curve all the way around the top and sides; when you come to the raw edges, tuck them under themselves and stitch them into place.

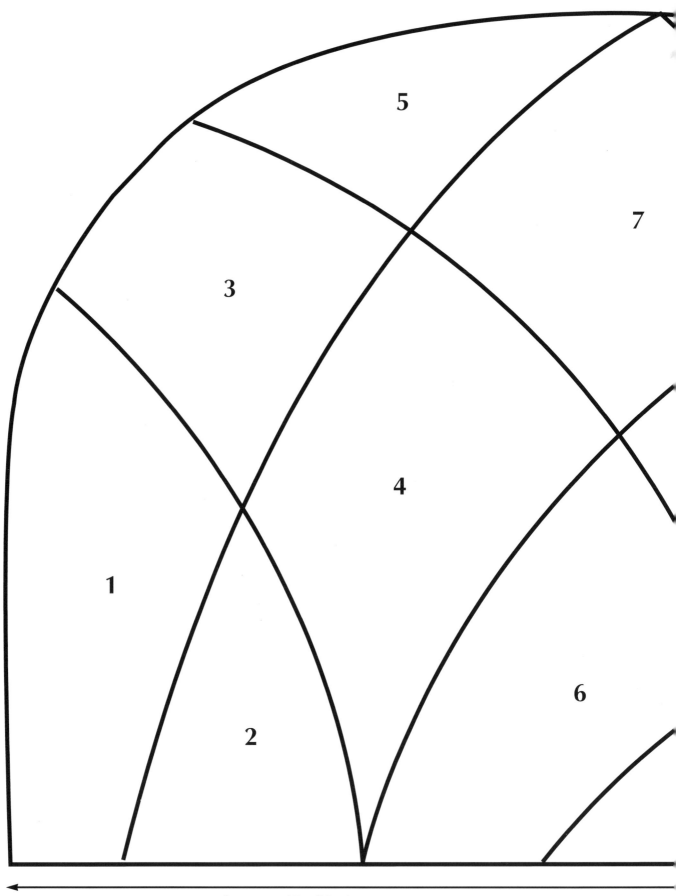

ENLARGE TO 15IN (38CM)

PROJECT 4: CLASSY TEACOSY

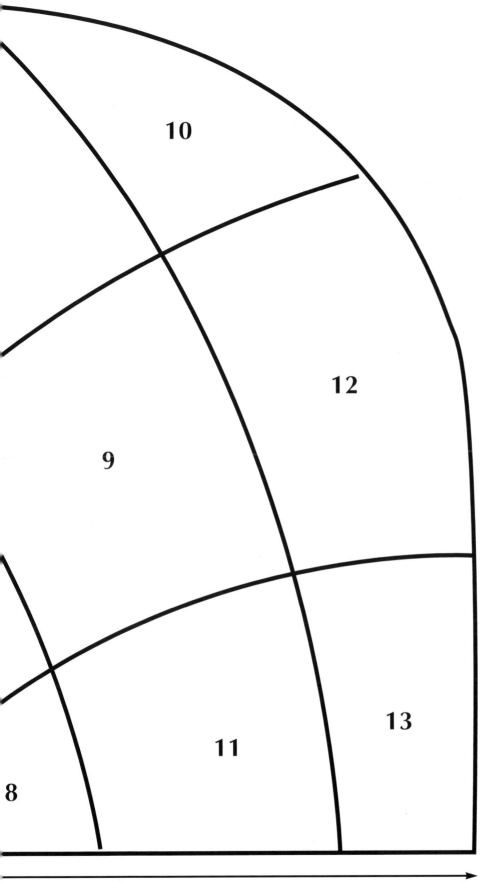

**STITCHING SEQUENCE:**

*All the lines of this design are added and stitched at the same stage.*

# Ammonite Mat

*The beautiful curved shapes of an ammonite are translated here into a striking mat for a dressing-table, bathroom or even dining table. Two shades of peach satin create the basic pattern, outlined with dark peach bias binding, but of course you could use cotton fabrics if you prefer. The inner strips of binding are all laid first, and this makes it easy to trap their raw ends under the main curve of the shell – the last line of binding to be added, all in one long strip.*

## PREPARATION

1   Enlarge the pattern on page 27 to the correct size, and go over the lines with a felt pen to make them darker.

2   Press the pale peach satin and lay it, right side up, over the enlarged pattern. Satin is quite slippery, so pin the two pieces together so that they don't slide about! Trace all the lines of the design onto the fabric (you don't need to write in the stars where marked – these are for the next stage), then unpin.

3   Turn the enlarged design over so that it's face down: you should be able to see the marked lines through the paper. If not, go over them again with the felt pen. Lay the fusing web, paper side up, over the pattern and trace the shapes of all the sections marked with a star. You can move the paper around to fit the shapes in; it doesn't matter which way they are facing.

4   Place the fusing web, web side down, onto the back of the mid-peach satin and press it with a warm iron to fuse it. Cut out the marked shapes along the pencil lines and peel off the backing paper from each section.

## MAKING UP

5   Lay the pale satin, marked side up, on a flat surface and put the mid-peach sections, right side up, in the correct positions on the design. Use an iron to fuse them into place.

6   Cut round the outline only of the ammonite shape and pin it into position on the right side of the table mat: make sure that there is a roughly even gap at each side, and that the shape is an even distance from the top and the bottom of the mat. Run a line of tacking or a line of small machine zigzag round the edges of the design and along the main curved line of the shell to make sure that the fabric stays in position while you add the bias binding.

7   Pin strips of bias binding along all the wiggly lines at the sides of the mid-peach pieces, and the three extra lines towards the centre of the ammonite; pull the binding into shape and press it as you go to set the curves. Tack the strips in place if you wish.

8   Stitch down both sides of each strip, by hand or machine, and trim off any stray threads or rough ends of bias binding.

MATERIALS
- One mid-peach table mat, at least 18 x 12in (46 x 30cm)
- Pale peach satin fabric, 18 x 12in (46 x 30cm)
- Mid-peach satin fabric, 9in (23cm) square
- Fusing web, 9in (23cm) square
- 4yd/4m Coats cotton bias binding in dark peach, 1/2in (12mm) wide when folded
- Matching Sylko or Drima sewing thread
- Soft pencil
- Paper, pencil, black felt pen etc for enlarging the pattern

## HANDY HINTS

*If you want to use the design for table linen, stitch several matching mats and buy toning plain napkins.*

*Satin may not be the most practical choice for table linen; try two tones of cotton fabric, or even two small prints that tone in with your decor, and pick a colour of bias binding that shows them off well.*

## STITCHING SEQUENCE:

**A** *Begin with all the wiggly lines bordering the mid-peach sections, plus the three solo wiggly lines near the centre of the shell.*

**B** *Now add the shell outline in one long line of binding, beginning where the bottom of the shell joins the main section, and taking the line all the way in to the centre in a spiral.*

**9** Beginning at the point where the bottom of the shell joins the main section, pin a single strip of bias binding all round the long curve of the shell, pressing as you go to set the curve. Towards the centre, where the curve gets very tight, run a gathering thread round the inner edge of the binding to help ease it into position. Tack the strip in position if you wish.

**10** Beginning at the same point as the binding, stitch along the inside edge of the curve first, by hand or machine. Make sure that you catch all the loose ends of the other bias strips securely under this one.

**11** Finally, stitch the outside curve of the long strip; when you come to the inner end of the binding at the centre of the shell, fold it under and stitch it into place so that it tapers into a neat point. If necessary, remove the gathering thread so that it doesn't show.

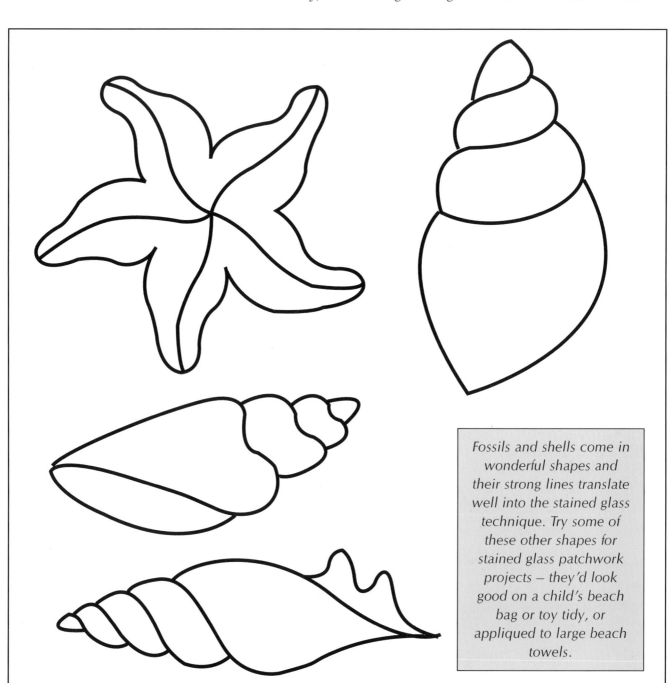

*Fossils and shells come in wonderful shapes and their strong lines translate well into the stained glass technique. Try some of these other shapes for stained glass patchwork projects – they'd look good on a child's beach bag or toy tidy, or appliqued to large beach towels.*

# Peacock Feather Curtain

## MATERIALS

- Long curtain in navy blue, at least 36in (92cm) wide
- Large scraps of nine different exotic fabrics (eg satins, silks and polyester silks, shot fabrics, brocades) in peacock colours – the largest piece, needed for the main green ring outside the eye of the feather, should be at least 18 x 12in (45 x 30cm)
- 5yd/5m of Coats navy blue satin bias binding, 3/4in (2cm) wide when folded
- Navy blue Drima or Sylko sewing thread
- Pale crayon, special marker for dark fabrics, or dressmakers' carbon paper in a light colour
- Paper, pencil, black felt pen etc for enlarging the pattern

*The wonderful colours and flowing lines of a peacock feather are captured in this simple design, used here to decorate the bottom of a curtain. Art Nouveau artists loved peacock feathers because of their sinuous lines and exotic sheen: the fabrics I've used for the design are silks, satins and shot polyesters, to try to capture the effect of the real thing! Finally the whole design is outlined in midnight blue satin bias binding, which catches the light and echoes the sheen on the fabrics.*

*Try to choose a sequence of fabrics that shades subtly through blue to green: if you don't have enough different colours, add some rich purple-blues at the bottom end of the feather.*

## Preparation

1   Enlarge the pattern on pages 30-31 to the correct size, and go over the lines with black felt pen to make them stronger. Write in the numbers of the pieces; these will help you identify which bit you are dealing with when you cut out the templates.

2   If you are making a matching pair of curtains, turn the drawing over and trace the design onto the second piece of paper: mark the relevant sections B1, B2 and so on, so that you don't get confused! Press all the coloured fabrics and the curtain.

## Making Up

3   Decide how far up the curtain you would like the design and mark the line with a fold or with pins. Lay the curtain over the tracing on a light-box and pin the two pieces together; trace the design onto the curtain using a pale crayon. Alternatively, you could use dressmakers' carbon paper in a pale colour for transferring the design. If you are making a second curtain, mark it using your mirror image copy of the design, making sure that you position it at the same height on the curtain.

4   Decide which fabric you will use for each piece. Try to put the colours in sequence so that they go from rich blue at the bottom of the feather, through turquoise and aquamarine part-way up, to shades of green round the 'eye' of the feather. If you are using shot

fabrics, you may find that these have different effects depending on which side of the fabric you use: see which one fits into your colour scheme best. Once you have decided on your fabric sequence, cut your drawn design into sections and use each piece as a template to cut the correct shape from the relevant fabric. You may find it less confusing to cut and position one piece at a time, working your way up the peacock feather, instead of cutting all the templates out together.

5   Put the pieces, right sides up, like a jigsaw puzzle over the traced design on your curtain, and check that you are happy with the way the different fabrics work together. If you are unhappy with any piece, re-cut it using a different piece of fabric. Once all the fabrics are in position, tack them carefully with small stitches: slippery fabrics like this tend to distort and move out of position very easily, so it's worth taking the time to anchor them securely. If you tack them round the very edges in navy blue, the tacking stitches will be hidden by the binding on the front and will be virtually invisible on the back of the curtain.

6   Begin positioning the bias binding, starting with the curved V-shape at the very bottom of the feather. You can do all of this with one piece: begin at one side of the feather and pleat the bias

ENLARGE TO 33IN (84CM)

**STITCHING SEQUENCE:**

**A** *Begin with the first curved V-shape at the bottom of the feather.*

**B** *Now add the second V-shape up from the bottom.*

**C** *Stitch the final curved V-shape.*

**D** *Add the two large pointed pear-shapes at the top of the feather – the very outside of the 'eye', and the next line in.*

**E** *Finally, add a continuous line round the centre of the 'eye' and down the middle of the feather to the end of the vein.*

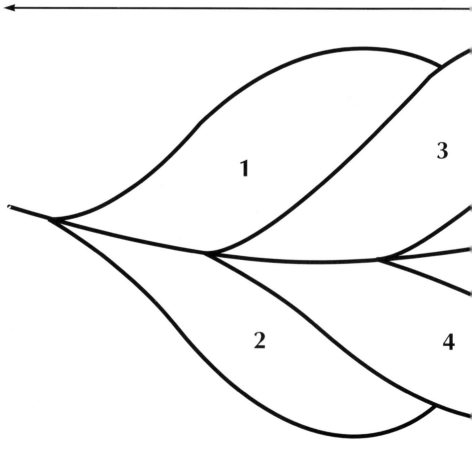

binding in the centre – the pleat will be covered later by the central vein. Press the line of binding to set the curves, tack it into position, then stitch this section in place by hand or machine.

7   Add the second V-shape in the same way, and then the third, pressing and stitching each curve individually before moving on to the next. Each curve encloses the raw ends of the previous one. Next, add the large pear shapes – round the outside of the eye, then the next line in from that. The raw ends from these shapes will be covered by the central vein of the feather.

8   Beginning at the point of the tiniest pear shape in the centre of the eye, lay a line of bias binding so that it goes round the central fabric piece, curves round to cover the raw end, and goes on down the centre of the feather to form the vein. At the bottom end, extend it slightly beyond the fabric pieces then fold the raw end under to make a neat end: stitch in place. Your curtain is now complete. Lay the appliqué section face down on a soft cloth, such as a towel, and press it gently from the back.

9   If you are making a matching curtain, construct it in exactly the same way, matching the fabrics for the corresponding pieces in the second peacock feather.

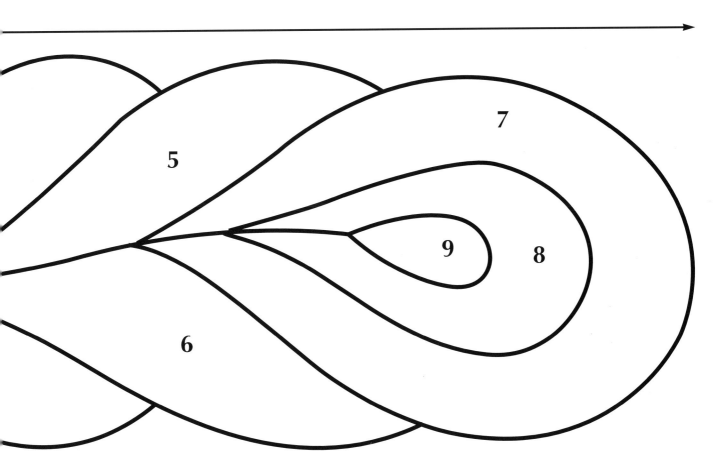

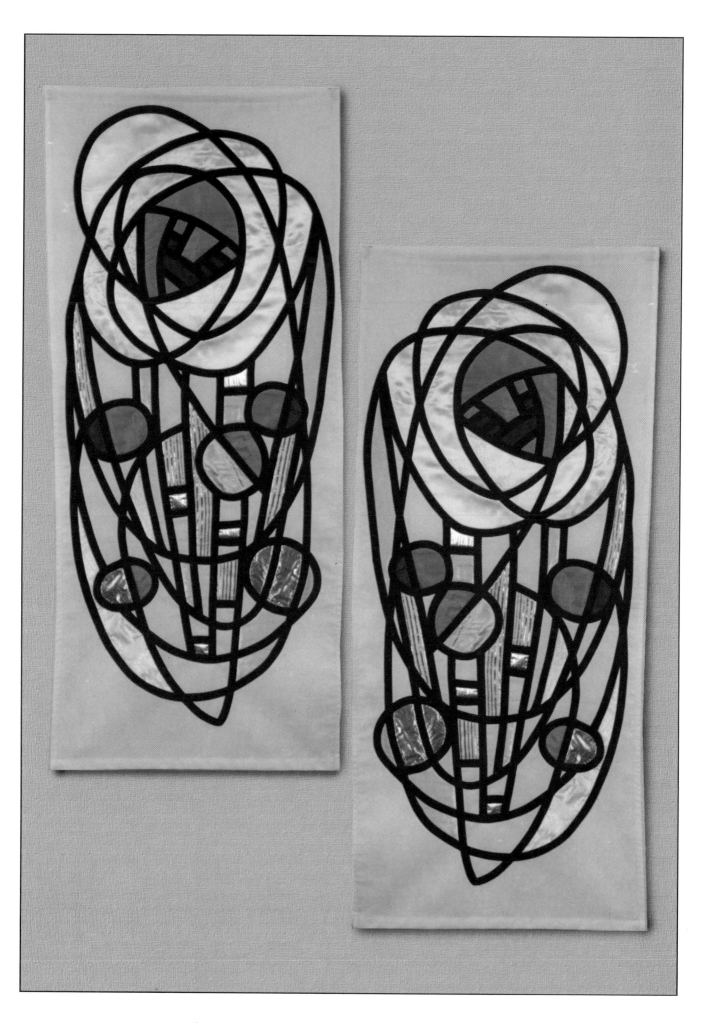

PROJECT 7: ART NOUVEAU ROSE WALL-HANGINGS

# PROJECT 7

# Art Nouveau Rose Wall-Hangings

*Charles Rennie Mackintosh, the leader of the Scottish branch of the Art Nouveau movement, used the stylised rose as his symbol in his stained glass, furniture and graphics. These elongated hangings are reminiscent of his long chair-backs and decorative glass panels.*

## PREPARATION

1 Enlarge the patterns on pages 34-35 and 36-37 to the correct size, and go over all the lines with black felt pen to make them stronger.

2 Press the pieces of backing fabric and lay one over each enlarged design, making sure that you have the designs at the same level on each piece: trace all the lines with pencil, and write the numbers in faintly.

## MAKING UP

3 Cut the numbered sections out along the marked lines to make templates; use these to cut patches out of the appropriate fabrics as marked on the keys. Put all the pieces inside the traced designs on the foundation pieces, assembling them like jigsaw puzzles, and tack them into place.

4 Now begin adding and stitching the bias binding outlines. Begin with all the small lines that cross the centres of the roses, and the short horizontal pieces under the flowers. Then continue building up the pattern in bias binding, pressing the curves with a steam iron to set them before you stitch, and following the stitching sequences with each pattern.

## FINISHING

5 Press the hangings. Fold and press a narrow double hem down both sides of each one, then stitch the hems into place, by hand or machine, using white thread.

6 Fold under $1/4$in (5mm) and then $1/2$in (10mm) at the top and bottom edges of each hanging, and stitch along the folded edges to make narrow casings. Slip the hanging rods through the casings.

## MATERIALS

- Two pieces of firm white fabric, such as sailcloth or cotton twill, 22 x 47in (55 x 120cm)
- Two pieces of pale pink satin, each at least 18in (45cm) square
- Scraps of mid pink, dark pink, silver, striped or figured silver, and opalescent fabrics
- 35yd/35m of Coats charcoal grey cotton bias binding, $1/2$in (12mm) wide when folded
- Drima or Sylko sewing thread in charcoal grey and white
- Four fine rods for hanging the finished pieces
- Paper, pencil, black felt pen etc for enlarging the pattern

### HANDY HINT
*When two or more adjoining pieces are in the same fabric, you don't need to cut them out individually; you can combine the shapes. So, for instance, all of the pale pink rose petals can be cut in one piece.*

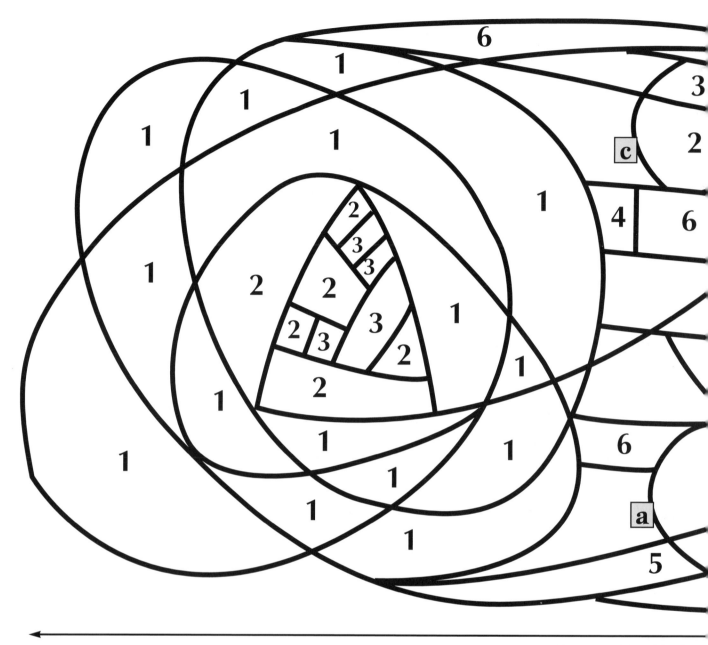

ENLARGE TO 39IN (99CM)

### STITCHING SEQUENCE:

**A** *Begin with the three shortest lines that cross the centre of the flower and the seven short horizontal bars in the rest of the design.*

**B** *Build up the bars inside the flower in sequence so that each one seals the raw edges of the previous one; finish with a curved triangle round the centre of the flower.*

**C** *Start a line at the bottom right of circle d; take it down to the bottom of the design then loop it up to the centre.*

**D** *Add the remaining seven vertical lines of different lengths near the centre of the design.*

**E** *Begin a long length of binding at the right-hand side of circle d, and take it across to the left of the flower centre, looping round the top of the flower twice, down the right-hand side and across the bottom of the whole design, and up to finish in a spiral round circle a.*

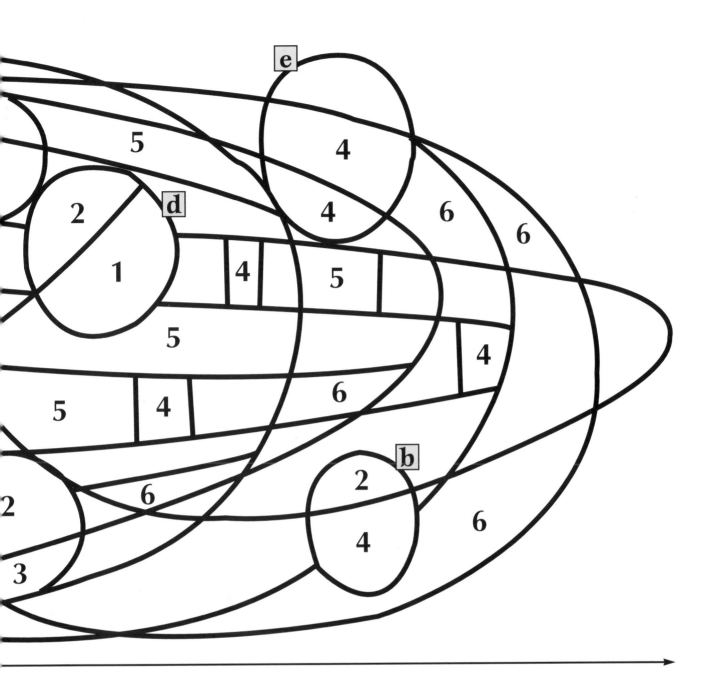

**F** *Add the curve that goes into the top of circle b, and another joining b and e*

**G** *Starting at the left-hand side of the main flower, take a pointed loop downwards and round to the side of circle c.*

**H** *Beginning at the same point again, take a long loop of binding round the lower edge*

*and right-hand side of the flower, back to the starting point, down to skim the left of circle a and the top of circle e, up the right-hand side, and a final trip round the flower to tuck under itself on the right-hand side.*

**I** *Finally, add circles of binding round b, c, d and e, tucking the raw ends in neatly.*

**KEY**

*Areas without numbers are the background fabric*

**1** Pale pink      **2** Mid pink
**3** Dark pink      **4** Silver
**5** Striped or figured silver
**6** Opalescent

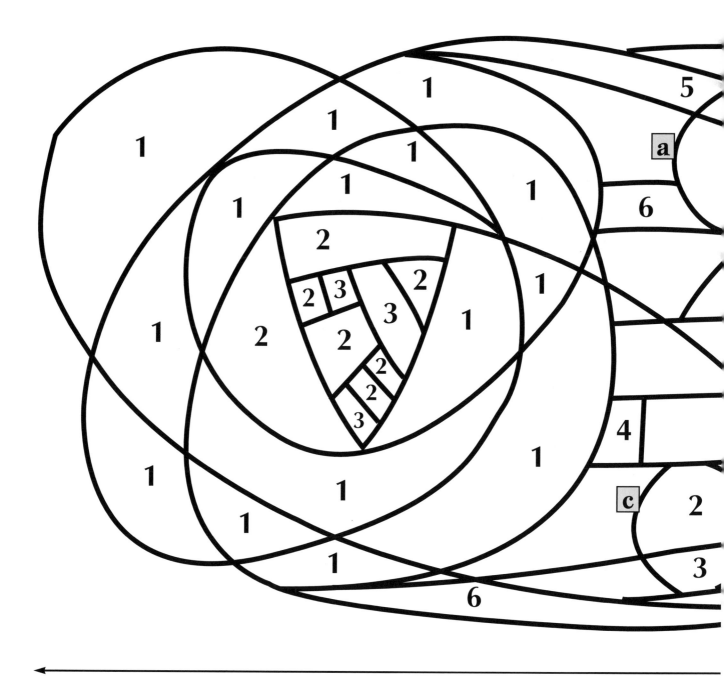

ENLARGE TO 39IN (99CM)

## STITCHING SEQUENCE:

**A** Begin with the three shortest lines that cross the centre of the flower and the seven short horizontal bars in the rest of the design.

**B** Build up the bars inside the flower in sequence so that each one seals the raw edges of the previous one; finish with a curved triangle round the centre of the flower.

**C** Start a line at the bottom left of circle d; take it down to the bottom of the design then loop it up to the centre.

**D** Add the remaining seven vertical lines of different lengths near the centre of the design.

**E** Begin a long length of binding at the left-hand side of circle d, and take it across to the right of the flower centre, looping round the top of the flower twice, down the left-hand side and across the bottom of the whole design, and up to finish in a spiral round circle a.

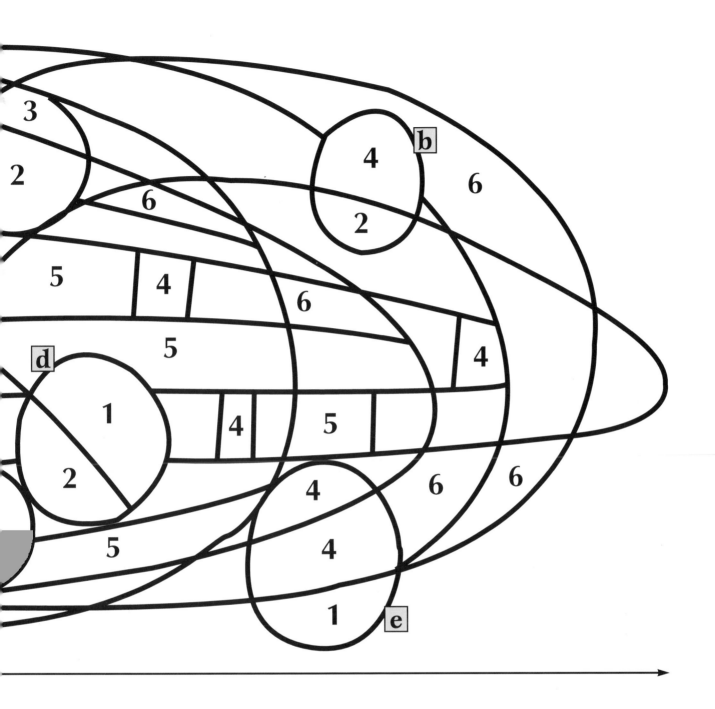

**F** Add the curve that goes into the top of circle b, and another joining b and e

**G** Starting at the right-hand side of the main flower, take a pointed loop downwards and round to the side of circle c.

**H** Beginning at the same point again, take a long loop of binding round the lower edge and left-hand side of the flower, back to the starting point, down to skim the right of circle a and the top of circle e, up the left-hand side, and a final trip round the flower to tuck under itself on the left-hand side.

**I** Finally, add circles of binding round b, c, d and e, tucking the raw ends in neatly.

**KEY**

*Areas without numbers are the background fabric*

**1** Pale pink  **2** Mid pink
**3** Dark pink  **4** Silver
**5** Striped or figured silver
**6** Opalescent

These designs are taken from
mediaeval stained glass
windows and Greek pottery,
and would all work well with
stained glass patchwork.

There's an Oriental influence in the designs on this page. Try the plum blossom design large as a dramatic wall-hanging, and the exotic butterfly and dragonfly as designs for cushion-covers. Try bold colour-schemes, edged in black or dark blue, or work with delicate pastels edged in white.

Floral designs have inspired textile artists for centuries – even millenia! The stylised lily on the left would work well in a square design, either a single large blossom or four smaller ones. The leafy branch could be repeated as a curtain edging, and the cornucopia shape could be filled with applique perse flowers and fruit cut from printed fabrics.

There's a traditional English, almost Jacobean flavour in this set of designs. The repeating swirl border on the left could be worked just with lines of fine binding, perhaps with different-coloured fabrics above and below the baseline. The acorns and oakleaves make attractive cornerpieces.

*More historical inspiration: pageantry and romance to the forefront! Use the pennant design with your own motif instead of the flower – perhaps a name, or an emblem that's significant to your family.*

Heraldic emblems from the days of chivalry were the inspiration for the designs here: shields, crests and stylised flowers. The rose would make a dramatic centrepiece for a quilt, and the border below would work well at any size.

Egyptian art is an endless source of inspiration: the crisp, clean lines and luminous colours are just asking to be translated into stained glass quilts ...The lotus border would make a wonderful bedhead, and the spiral border can be extended as far as you wish.

The Art Deco era was itself inspired by Egyptian art: the discovery of Tutankhamen's tomb came at its height, and encouraged the flowering of geometric designs such as the ones here. Stars, triangles, lightning flashes and segments of circles make strong, bold patterns that work perfectly for stained glass patchwork.

*Inspiration for the designs on this page came from the mosaics at Ravenna – a feast of bright colour and line. Each of these patterns can be used as a border, or built up into an all-over pattern by using the design in a regular grid. Try them at different sizes, for everything from a tablecloth border to a full-size quilt.*

There's really no limit to the patterns you can use for stained glass patchwork: any design with bold, clear lines, such as these abstract shapes, will work well. Experiment with different colour-schemes and colours of binding, to see how radically varied the same design can look.

# Bethlehem Scene

## MATERIALS

- One piece of double-sided fusing web, 18in (45cm) square
- One piece of firm black backing fabric, such as cotton, twill or sailcloth etc, 20in (50cm) square
- 7yd/7m of Coats bias binding, cotton or satin, $1/2$in (12mm) wide when folded
- Black Sylko or Drima sewing thread
- Large scraps of 12-15 different metallic fabrics – the largest pieces need to be 18 x 6in (46 x 15cm) for the sky, and 10in (25cm) square for the central building
- Soft pencil, and white pencil or pale marker for dark fabrics
- Large star sequin
- Metallic thread for stitching on the sequin
- Paper, pencil etc for enlarging the pattern

*These striking wall-hangings look like stained glass windows: the jewel-bright colours of the metallic fabrics catch the light and reflect the sparkle of the Christmas season. The photograph shows how exactly the same design can look totally different, depending on what fabrics you use and how you position them in relation to each other.*

*Make a Bethlehem hanging as a seasonal decoration for your home or to give away as a Christmas present, or make a larger version for use in a church or school: the shiny fabrics will look wonderful during a candle-lit service. Because metallic fabrics can be tricky to work with, this project uses bonding web to fuse the cut shapes to the background – this stops them from moving around, and also prevents them from fraying.*

## PREPARATION

1  Enlarge the pattern on page 50 to the correct size, and draw in all the numbers as marked. (You'll notice that the pattern is a mirror image of the finished scene: this is because all the pieces of web will be put onto the backs of the fabrics, and so will be reversed.)

2  Lay the fusing web, paper side up, over the enlarged pattern and trace all the lines and numbers onto the paper. Cut out the marked pieces carefully.

## MAKING UP

3  Decide which metallic fabric you will use for each part of the design. Choose the piece for the sky first, as this is the largest section and will dominate the scene. When you've chosen it, lay the fabric right side down on the ironing board, and lay the piece of fusing web marked 1 onto the back of the fabric, paper side up. Press the paper shape with a warm iron to fuse it onto the fabric. Continue in the same way with the other shapes.

4  Cut carefully round the edges of the fusing web pieces. Put the pieces together, right sides up, like a jigsaw puzzle and check that you are happy with the way the different fabrics work together. (Remember that each pair of fabrics will be separated by black bias binding, so it doesn't matter if the colours appear to clash!) If you are unhappy with any section, re-cut it using a new piece of web and fabric.

ENLARGE TO 18IN (45CM) SQUARE

## HANDY HINT

*Metallic fabrics are expensive to buy, but often you can obtain them from unsuspected sources! Look out in charity shops for evening blouses made in lamé or similar fabrics, and try metallic ribbons for some of the smaller sections of the design.*

PROJECT 8: BETHLEHEM SCENE

**5** Lay the black backing fabric on a flat surface, right side down, and position your drawing on top so that there is an even margin of black fabric all the way around. Using the white pencil or fabric marker, draw round the edges of the paper to mark an 18in (45cm) square. (You don't need to transfer all the lines of the design: the marked square will be enough.)

**6** Peel the backing paper off the sky piece and position it, right side up, on the backing square so that the top and side edges align. Fuse it in place with a warm iron; place the iron flat on the fabric, rather than using a to-and-fro movement; this helps to prevent the pieces from moving out of position. Continue working down the design, fusing the pieces in position in the same way.

**7** Beginning at the right-hand edge of the castle wall, lay a piece of bias binding over the join between the sky and the castle wall and pin it in place. When you come to a corner, fold the binding crisply to make a right angle; continue to the top of the large dome and cut the binding. Pin pieces of binding over the large and small doorways and the pointed dome at the top of the tower, the top two steps of the staircase, and the small dome near the bottom of the design, pulling the curves into shape and folding any corners or points crisply. Press the lines of binding with a steam iron to set their shapes.

**8** Set your sewing machine to a small zigzag, and thread it with black cotton. Stitch the inside of each curve or shape first, catching down the edge of the binding and a small section of fabric, then stitch the outside edges.

**9** In the same way, add binding to the large dome, and the top and edge of the small building marked number 13.

**10** Next, add binding to the top and small right-hand edge of the central building. Do the dome on the right of the design, then the building underneath it. Use one long strip to work along the top and down the side of the tower, and to finish off the staircase right to the bottom of the design.

**11** Finally, outline each window shape in the centre. Begin each strip of binding at the bottom left corner, take it up to a crisp point and down the other side; fold it at the bottom right corner and take it back to the start. Cut it slightly wider than the bottom of the window and fold the raw end under so that it tucks out of sight, then stitch the binding in the usual way.

## FINISHING

**12** Fold the edges of the backing fabric over in an even double hem all the way around the edges of the design, and stitch in place.

**13** Stitch the sequin in position in the sky, using the metallic thread. Make two small hanging loops from binding and attach them to the back of the scene at the top corners.

### STITCHING SEQUENCE:

**A** Begin with the castle wall at the top of the design, the two pointed doorways (9 and 11), the top two steps of the staircase, the pointed dome at the top of the tower (5), and the small dome near the bottom of the design (12).

**B** Now add the large dome (3) under the castle wall, and the top and left-hand edge of the small building at the centre bottom (13).

**C** Next, bind the top and tiny right-hand edge of the large central building (4).

**D** Now you can do the smaller dome (7) to the right of the design.

**E** Finish off the building on the right (8) by covering its top and left-hand edge. Use one long line of binding to cover the top and right-hand edge of the tower (6), and take the same strip down the remaining parts of the staircase to outline piece 10.

**F** Finally, do the window-frames (14 and 15) in the centre of the design.

# PROJECT 9

# Iris Wall-Hanging

*Irises bloom in all their beauty on this magnificent wall-hanging:
I've used shiny fabrics throughout to give an opulence to the
whole design; try silks, satins, shot fabrics and metallics
to catch the light.*

## PREPARATION

1 Enlarge the pattern on pages 54-55 to the correct size, and draw in all the numbers as marked. Go over the lines of the design with black felt pen to make them stronger.

2 Press the cream satin fabric and lay it, right side up, over the enlarged drawing: pin the two together, as the satin tends to slither! Trace the design onto the satin in pale crayon, and unpin.

## MAKING UP

3 Cut out the numbered sections and use these as templates to cut shapes from the appropriate fabrics. Position them on the background fabric and tack them securely in place.

4 Beginning with the leaf sections going up from the bottom of the design, and the sections of pale leaf above the bottom and middle flowers, lay binding in place and stitch it in position by hand or machine.

5 Now add binding to all the sections of the inner frame.

6 Add the tips of all the leaves, the stems of the flowers, and then the large leaf in the centre. Fold the binding crisply to make good points at the leaf tips.

7 Work each iris flower in the same order, following the stitching sequence on page 54. Press the design on the reverse.

## FINISHING

8 Lay the black backing fabric on a flat surface and position the dolmette in the centre. Cover the dolmette with the stained glass design, right side up, then pin, tack and stitch through all layers round the edge of the design (the frame, leaf tips and petals where they overlap) to quilt it slightly.

9 Fold the backing fabric over to the front in an even double hem, and stitch in position. Make three hanging loops from binding and stitch them in place at even intervals across the top.

MATERIALS
- One piece of cream satin fabric, 40 x 27in (102 x 68cm)
- One piece of dolmette or curtain lining, 40 x 27in (102 x 68cm)
- One piece of black backing fabric, 42 x 29in (107 x 73cm)
- Roughly 17yd/17m of Coats bias binding in black, 1/2in (12mm) wide when folded
- Black Sylko or Drima sewing thread
- Large scraps of exotic fabrics in three shades of green for the leaves – the largest piece, of the middle shade, needs to be 26 x 8in (66 x 20cm)
- Scraps of exotic fabrics in four shades of mauve or purple, plus one yellow or gold, for the flowers
- Crayon in a pale colour
- Paper, pencil, black felt pen etc for enlarging the pattern

## HANDY HINT
*Dolmette is a particular
kind of wadding, firmer
and heavier than ordinary
polyester wadding.
If you can't find dolmette,
use a piece of curtain
interlining or a layer of
thick fabric – or cut a
section from an unwanted
blanket.*

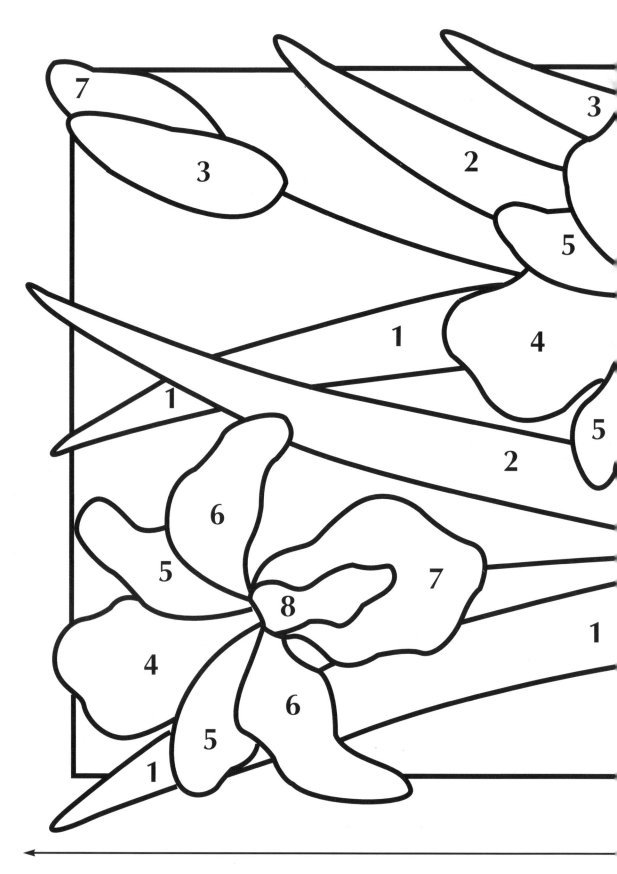

## STITCHING SEQUENCE:

**A** *Begin with the leaf bases, and the pale leaf sections above the bottom and middle flowers.*

**B** *Now add the flower stems and the leaf tips.*

**C** *Next, outline the large leaf in the centre of the design.*

**D** *Now you can put in all the different sections of the straight lines framing the design; make sure that you keep the frame as straight as possible.*

PROJECT 8: IRIS WALL-HANGING

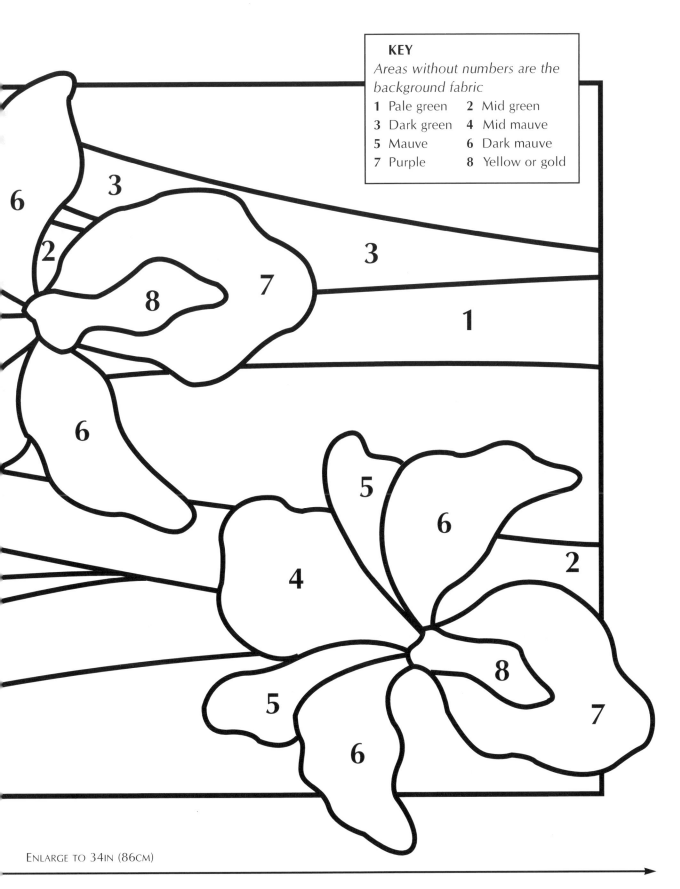

KEY

*Areas without numbers are the background fabric*

1 Pale green    2 Mid green
3 Dark green    4 Mid mauve
5 Mauve    6 Dark mauve
7 Purple    8 Yellow or gold

ENLARGE TO 34IN (86CM)

**E** *Work each flower in the same order. Begin by outlining the yellow central part and the very top petal of each one.*

**F** *Now use one piece of binding on each flower to go round one top wing, around the bottom petal, and back up round the other top wing.*

**G** *Finally, finish each flower with a figure-eight section going round the two bottom wings and tucking under itself in the centre to conceal the raw ends*

# PROJECT 10

# African-Style Sofa Throw

*Bright plain fabrics and bold safari-style prints give a hint of Africa to this stylish sofa throw. Even though it's quite large, it's extremely easy – and quite quick – to make; you could complete the whole project in an evening!*

## MATERIALS

- One piece of white or cream calico or sheeting, 44in (112cm) square
- One piece of firm black backing fabric, 46in (118cm) square
- About 13yd/13m of Coats bias binding in black, 1/2in (12mm) wide when folded
- Black Sylko or Drima sewing thread
- Large scraps of 16-20 different bright fabrics, plain and patterned – the largest piece, for the long panel to the right of the centre, needs to be 44 x 10in (112 x 25cm)
- Soft pencil
- Paper, pencil, black felt pen etc for enlarging the pattern

## PREPARATION

1  Enlarge the pattern on pages 58-59 to the correct size, and go over all the lines with black felt pen to make them stronger. Draw in all the numbers as marked.

2  Lay the white foundation fabric over the enlarged design, and trace all the lines with pencil. Write the numbers in faintly, too.

## MAKING UP

3  Decide which fabric you will use for each part of the design. Choose the four large pieces going down the centre first; select a range of different colours and tones, and a mixture of plain and patterned fabrics. Then choose colours for each of the smaller pieces in the same way, checking that they look good against each other and provide a mixture of tones and patterns across the throw.

4  When you are sure of your colours, cut along the different lines of the design and use these pieces as templates for cutting the fabrics. Put all the pieces inside the marked design on the foundation square, assembling them like a jigsaw puzzle.

5  Now begin adding and stitching the bias binding outlines. Begin with the two squiggly lines down the centre, and all the short straight lines down the right-hand side. Then add the final squiggly line, and build up the rainbow-shaped curves from the top downwards. Finish with the last two long straight lines.

## FINISHING

6  Lay the black backing fabric on a flat surface, right side down, and position the stained glass square on top so that there is an even margin of black fabric all the way around. Fold the edges of the backing fabric over in an even double hem all the way around the edges of the design, and stitch in place to complete your sofa throw.

## STITCHING SEQUENCE:

**A** *Begin with the two long squiggly lines that run down the central panel of the design.*

**B** *Now add all the short straight lines down the right-hand side of the design.*

**C** *Next, cover the third squiggly line.*

**D** *Now you can put in all the rainbow-shaped curves; begin with the top one and work downwards.*

**E** *Finish with the final two long, straight lines down the outsides of the central panel.*

### VARIATIONS

*If you want to keep the African feel of the sofa throw but in more muted colours, try plains and prints in safari colours such as beige, rust, earth browns, forest greens and maroons: you may even be able to get some jungle prints. Bind the design in dark brown or green.*

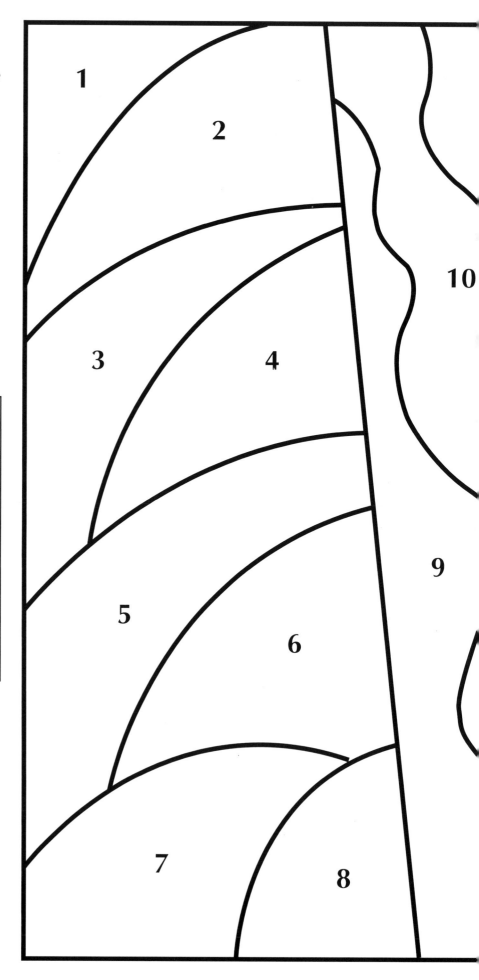

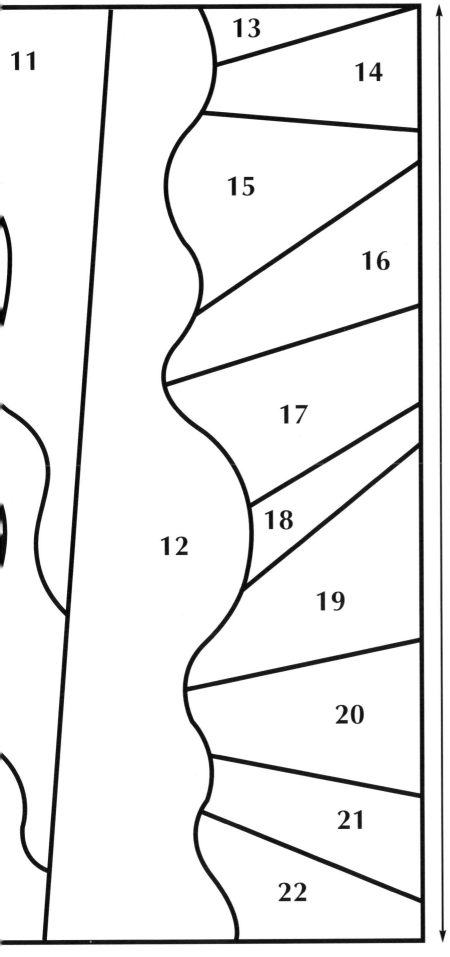

## HANDY HINTS

*Use a white or cream fabric for the foundation: if you use black or any other dark colour, it will show through the paler patches such as the yellow.*

*The size of this throw has been cunningly designed so that you can fit the enlarged pattern onto one sheet of dressmakers' tracing paper! That saves having to join lots of smaller sheets of paper to create the required size.*

# PROJECT 11

# Holly Banner

*Christmas wouldn't be the same without holly, but sometimes it's hard to find the real thing. Now you can create your own holly decoration, which will become a favourite part of your Christmas celebrations year after year.*

## PREPARATION

1 Enlarge the pattern on pages 62-63 to the correct size, and go over all the lines with black felt pen to make them stronger. Draw in all the numbers as marked.

2 Lay the pale green foundation fabric over the enlarged design, and trace all the lines with pencil. Write the numbers in faintly, too – don't draw them too boldly, or they may show through some of the lighter fabric patches.

## MAKING UP

3 Cut the numbered pattern pieces along the marked lines, section by section, to make templates; use these to cut patches out of the appropriate fabrics as marked on the key. Put all the pieces inside the marked design on the foundation piece, assembling them like a jigsaw puzzle, and tack them in position.

4 Now begin adding and stitching the bias binding outlines. On this design it's not always immediately obvious which lines should be worked first, so follow the stitching sequence on page 62 carefully. As the final part of this sequence, tack the rectangle of binding round the inner edge of the frame, but don't stitch it yet.

## FINISHING

5 Lay the Christmas check or print backing fabric on a flat surface, right side down, and lay the wadding on top so that there is an even margin of fabric all around. Position the stained glass square on top of the wadding, and pin or tack the three layers together at intervals. Stitch the tacked binding on in the normal way; this time you will be stitching through all layers, which will quilt the banner slightly.

6 Fold the edges of the backing fabric over in an even single hem all the way around the edges of the panel, and pin in place. Seal the raw edges with a border of bias binding, then make three hanging loops from binding and stitch them to the top at regular intervals.

## MATERIALS

- One piece of very pale green cotton fabric or sheeting, 33 x 24in (84 x 61cm)
- One piece of cotton fabric in a Christmas check or print, 35 x 26in (89 x 66cm)
- One piece of 2oz wadding, 34 x 25in (87 x 63.5cm)
- About 16yd/16m of Coats cotton bias binding in dark green, 1/2in (12mm) wide when folded
- Dark green Sylko or Drima sewing thread
- Large scraps of pale green cotton fabric, slightly darker than your foundation fabric
- Large scraps of plain cotton fabric in three different tones of mid or dark green
- Large scraps of two slightly different plain red cotton fabrics
- Soft pencil
- Paper, pencil, black felt pen etc for enlarging the pattern

### HANDY HINT

*As it takes quite a time to build up this design, you may find it helpful to hold the patches in place on the foundation fabric with lines of zigzag instead of having to tack them all.*

## STITCHING SEQUENCE:

**A** *Begin with the line going down the left and top edges of the upper holly leaf; you can create this with two loops of the same line of binding.*

**B** *Using one long piece of binding, begin at the top centre of the design, at the outer edge of the frame. Outline the top vein of the upper leaf, then down its right-hand side to become the bottom vein of the bottom leaf – and out to the lower left-hand corner of the frame.*

**C** *Now do the top vein of the lower leaf, and the central vein of the upper leaf.*

**D** *Outline the upper right curve of the top leaf; this curve begins and ends in the frame.*

**E** *Bind both left-hand edges of the lower leaf and its central vein, then add the line along its bottom edge and into the frame.*

**F** *Do the short curve from the top left corner down to the berries, then add the long line that goes from the top left-hand corner of the frame, through the bottom vein of the upper leaf and out to the right-hand edge. Continue this line down to the single berry and to the edge of the frame.*

**G** *Add the line from the two berries round the final edge of the lower leaf, then the one from the left of the berries along the bottom of the upper leaf.*

**H** *Outline all the berries, beginning with the one that's only part-visible.*

**I** *Add the inner frame outline.*

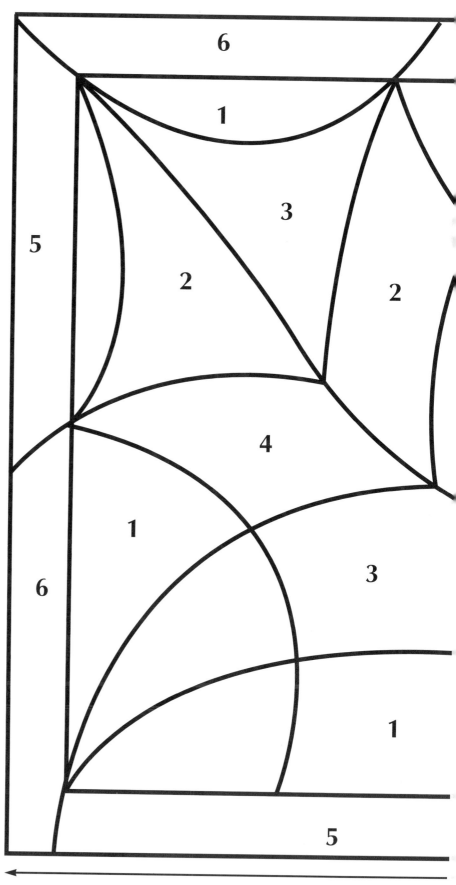

ENLARGE TO 33IN (84CM)

PROJECT 11: HOLLY BANNER

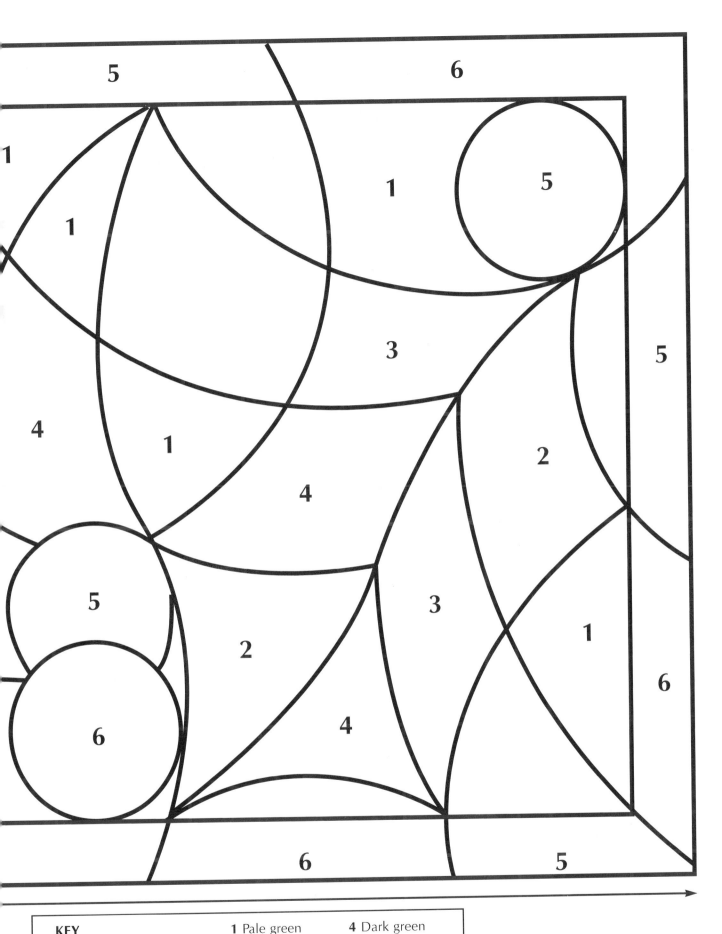

**KEY**
*Areas without numbers are the background fabric*

| | |
|---|---|
| **1** Pale green | **4** Dark green |
| **2** Mid green | **5** Red |
| **3** Mid/dark green | **6** Dark red |

# PROJECT 12

# Cheerful Clown

## MATERIALS

- One piece of thick cream or white furnishing fabric, 31 x 51in (80 x 130cm)
- About 5yd/5m Coats cotton bias binding in bright blue, 1in (2.5cm) wide when folded
- Coats cotton bias binding in different bright colours, 1/2in (12mm) wide when folded; you will need about 13yd/13m in total
- Sylko or Drima sewing thread in bright colours to match the bias bindings, plus black
- Large scraps of lots of different cotton fabrics in bright plain colours and bold prints; the largest piece, for the trousers, needs to be 16in (41cm) square
- 1yd/1m narrow ribbon for the balloon strings, any colour
- 1yd/1m bright patterned ribbon for the shoe ties, 5/8in (15mm) wide
- Two large buttons
- One artificial flower
- Soft pencil
- Paper, pencil, black felt pen etc for enlarging the pattern

---

### HANDY HINT

*This is an excellent project for using up all those odd lengths of binding left over from previous projects!*

---

*Every child loves a clown, and this one will be no exception! This design shows that you don't need to stick to the same colour of bias binding throughout a project: the different colours enhance the effect – so do the 'added extras' such as the real buttons, ribbon bows, and a flower on the clown's hat.*

## PREPARATION

1   Enlarge the pattern on pages 66-67 to the correct size, and go over all the lines with black felt pen to make them stronger.

2   Lay the furnishing fabric over the enlarged design, and trace all the lines with pencil.

## MAKING UP

3   Decide which fabric you are going to have where on the design: aim for as much contrast from piece to piece as possible. When you have decided, cut the enlarged pattern along the marked lines, section by section, to make templates; use these to cut patches out of the appropriate fabrics. Put all the pieces inside the marked design on the foundation piece, assembling them like a jigsaw puzzle, and tack them in place.

4   Now begin adding and stitching the bias binding outlines. Once again, aim for as much contrast as possible – so, if you have a red gingham patch for instance, outline it with blue or green. Follow the stitching sequence on page 66 for the order.

5   Stitch the narrow ribbon in a V-shape to make the strings for the balloons: you can tuck the raw ends of the ribbon into the binding round the balloons. Tie bows in the patterned ribbon and stitch them to the shoes. Stitch the buttons on the ends of the braces, and the artificial flower to the hat. Use hand or machine embroidery, fused fabric patches or a mixture to create features.

## FINISHING

6   Fold the edges of the foundation fabric over in an even single hem all the way around the edges of the panel, and pin in place. Seal the raw edges with a border of wide bias binding, taking the binding right out to the fold, and stitch it securely down both sides. Finally, make six hanging loops from different colours of bias binding and stitch them to the top at regular intervals.

## STITCHING SEQUENCE:

**A** *Begin by outlining the bobble at the top of the hat, the right-hand balloon, the edges of the socks, and the square patches on the trousers.*

**B** *Now add the binding round the shoes (tucking the raw ends in neatly), the cone of the hat, and the shoulders and edges of the shirt.*

**C** *Outline the hands, pleating the*

*binding at the thumbs, and add the edges of the trousers all round.*

**D** *Stitch the binding round the braces and the cuffs; finish the raw ends of the cuff bindings*

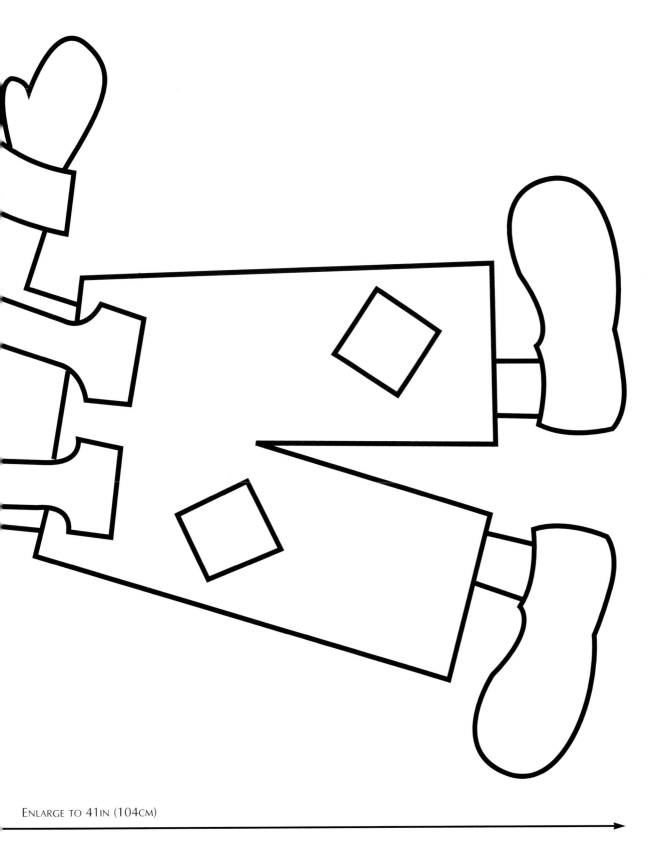

ENLARGE TO 41IN (104CM)

neatly by turning them under
themselve before stitching.

**E** Add two curved lines round the
knot of the bow tie, then
complete the outline with one
line of binding.

**F** Work lines of machine satin
stitch or zigzag round the hair
sections, then add a line of bias
binding round the face.

**G** Complete the design with the
oval shape round the hat brim;

if you position the raw ends
carefully, you can cover them
with the flower when you stitch
it on!

**H** Add the facial features, buttons,
ribbons and flower.

# PROJECT 13

# Garland Tablecloth

*Orange and green make a striking colour-scheme, and what could be better to show it off than a garland of oranges and their leaves? I've designed this pattern cunningly so that you use the same tracing four times, once in each quarter of the cloth.*

## PREPARATION

1   Enlarge the pattern on pages 70-71 to the correct size, and go over all the lines with black felt pen to make them stronger. Draw in all the numbers as marked.

2   Fold the cloth very accurately in quarters, and press the folds to set them. Lay one quarter over the enlarged design, matching the fold lines to the straight edges around the pattern and making sure that the correct part of the pattern is towards the outside of the cloth. Trace all the lines with pencil. Repeat with each of the quarters in turn, making sure that the pattern matches up at each end. Write the numbers in faintly.

## MAKING UP

3   Cut the enlarged pattern along the marked lines, section by section, to make templates; use each template to cut four patches out of the appropriate fabric as marked on the key. Pin all the pieces inside the marked design on the foundation piece as you cut them, assembling them like a jigsaw puzzle. As there are lots of pieces involved, you may want to hold them in place with lines of zigzag to stop them moving while you add the binding.

4   Now begin adding and stitching the bias binding outlines. Start with the central veins of all the leaves; press the binding to make it hold the S-shaped curves, and stitch each central vein in place down both sides.

5   Choose any place around the garland to start the next stage, and begin adding the binding around the oranges. The curves are quite tight, but pressing with a steam iron will loosen the weave enough to give you the curve you want. Pin all the orange outlines in place, but only stitch the inside curves of each line of binding; then you can tuck raw ends from other lines of binding under the outer curves.

6   Add the lengths of binding round the edges of the leaves in the same way, just stitching the inside edges. When all the pieces of binding are in place, stitch round the outer edges of the leaves and the oranges, working anti-clockwise round the garland.

MATERIALS
- One peach tablecloth, 48in (122cm) square plus fringe
- About 18yd/18m Coats cotton bias binding in dark brown, 1/2in (12mm) wide when folded
- Sylko or Drima sewing thread in dark brown
- Fat quarters of plain cotton fabric in mid green, dark green, mid orange and dark orange
- Soft pencil
- Paper, pencil, black felt pen etc for enlarging the pattern

## HANDY HINT
*Because there are so many small sections and it will take you quite a while to add the binding, you may prefer to fuse the fabrics in place with bonding web. Remember, though, that this will stiffen your cloth, so choose a fairly substantial one to begin with.*

**STITCHING SEQUENCE:**

**A** *Begin with all the veins down the centres of the leaves; each vein has an s-curve.*

**B** *Now add the binding round all the oranges, but only stitch the inside curves of these pieces.*

**C** *Next, add all the bindings round the leaves; again, only stitch the inside edges of these sections.*

**D** *Finally, stitch the outside edges of all the orange and leaf outlines, working anti-clockwise round the garland.*

## VARIATIONS

*You could do this design just as effectively on a pale green background, or a lemon yellow one for a summery look.*

*For autumn, turn the oranges into apples and stitch them in two shades of red fabric on a tan background, or work an apple garland on white or a seasonal print for your Christmas table.*

PROJECT 13: GARLAND TABLECLOTH

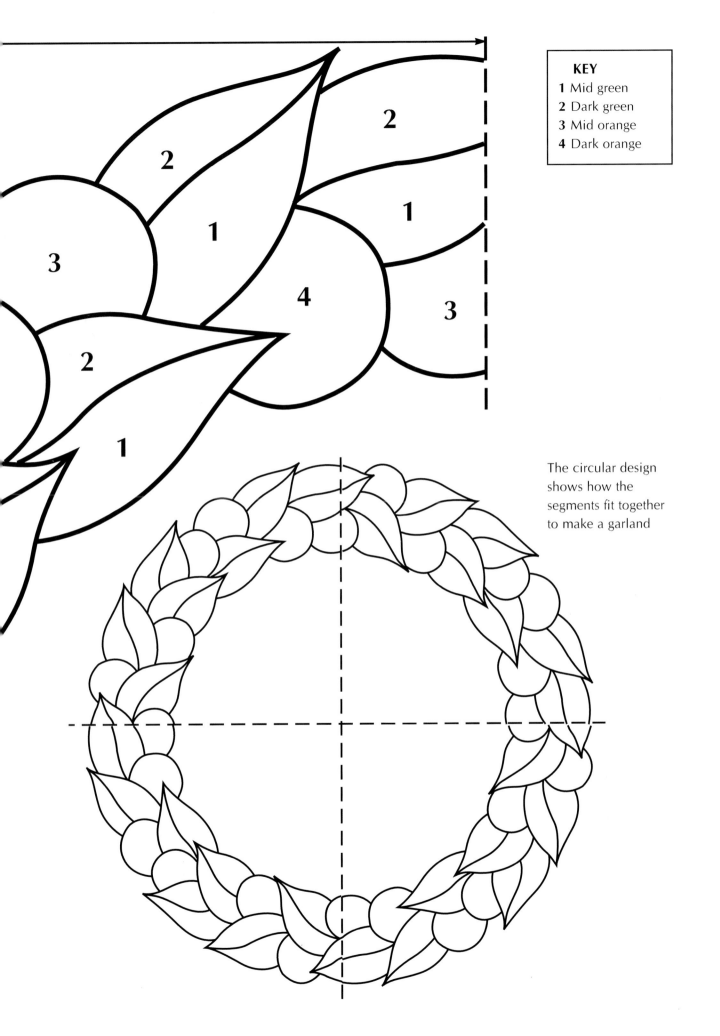

The circular design
shows how the
segments fit together
to make a garland

**PROJECT 13: GARLAND TABLECLOTH**

# Lotus Floor Cushion

## MATERIALS

- Two pieces of pale yellow sheeting, 48in (122cm) square
- Two pieces of white or cream calico or sheeting, 47in (120cm) square
- About 18yd/18m Coats cotton bias binding in dark blue, 1in (2.5cm) wide when folded
- Sylko or Drima sewing threads in dark blue, yellow and cream
- Half a yard/metre of mid blue plain cotton fabric, about 24in (60cm) square
- Pale blue plain cotton fabric, about 9in (23cm) square
- Half a yard/metre of very pale blue plain cotton fabric
- One yard/metre of blue print cotton fabric
- Half a yard/metre of dark yellow cotton fabric
- 24in (60cm) yellow zip fastener
- Soft pencil
- Paper, pencil, black felt pen, dressmaker's tracing paper etc for enlarging the pattern
- Polystyrene beads or flame-retardant foam chips for filling

*A giant Egyptian lotus flower makes the perfect design for a large square floor cushion, big enough to curl up on for a snooze! The Egyptians used a lot of turquoise, lapis lazuli and gold in their work – think of Tutankhamen's mask; I've echoed this by creating the lotus flower in an unusual colour-scheme of yellow and several different blues, outlined with dark blue binding.*

*You could choose any colour-scheme that complements your own decor: just substitute fabrics of varying tones in suitable amounts, and make sure that you select a colour of bias binding that draws them together visually.*

## PREPARATION

1 Enlarge the pattern on page 75 to the correct size, and go over all the lines with black felt pen to make them stronger. Draw in all the numbers as marked.

2 Press the pale yellow foundation fabric and lay it over the enlarged design; trace all the lines in pencil. Mark the numbers in very lightly, in case they show through any of the paler patches.

## MAKING UP

3 Cut the enlarged pattern along the marked lines, section by section, to make templates; use each template to cut a patch out of the appropriate fabric as marked on the key. Pin all the pieces inside the marked design on the foundation piece as you cut them, assembling them like a jigsaw puzzle. As there are lots of pieces involved, you may want to hold them in place with lines of zigzag to stop them moving while you add the binding; if you don't want to zigzag them, tack them securely.

4 Now begin adding and stitching the bias binding outlines. Start with the four short sections on the inner curves of the long outside ring, and the lower curve nearest the base of the flower.

5 Add the binding round the two large and two small background petals, pleating the points neatly. Press the curves to set them before you stitch the binding in place.

6 Next, outline the central large petal and its small counterpart, pleating the points neatly and taking the binding down into the top lines of the marked rings.

## STITCHING SEQUENCE:

**A** *Begin with the small curves on the inside edge of the outer ring, and the plain curve nearest the base of the flower.*

**B** *Now add the binding round the four background petals – two large and two small.*

**C** *Next, outline the two central petals – one large and one small.*

**D** *Bind the inside curves only of the outer petals – two large and two small.*

**E** *Complete the remaining three rings across the flower, and its top curve.*

**F** *Bind the outsider of the flower shape from the top of one petal, down round the base, to the tip of the petal at the opposite corner.*

**G** *Now add all the short strips between the different sections of the border; you don't need to do the strips at the corners.*

**H** *Finally, stitch four straight lengths of binding down the inner edges of the border.*

**7** Now add the binding along the inner curves of the four outer petals – two large and two small. Don't bind the outsides of these shapes – that will be done when the flower is outlined.

**8** Add the remaining curved lines above and below the petals. With the outer ring of the flower, finish the curved line just when it joins the straight edge of the border – don't carry it all the way to the corners.

**9** To complete the flower shape, attach one long line of binding from the tip of one outside petal, down round the base and up to the other petal tip. Make sure that you have an even curve going round each side of the base.

**10** Now cut short strips of binding to go between the sections on the border, and attach these. You don't need to do the short lines at each corner; these will be covered by the next stage.

**11** As the final stage in adding the binding, lay long straight strips along the inner edges and stitch them into position down both sides: as the binding has a tendency to curve, make sure that you keep it in straight lines.

## Finishing

**12** Press the second piece of pale yellow sheeting and lay it right side up on a flat surface; position the stained glass design, right side down, on the top and tack round all the edges, half an inch (1cm) from the raw edges. Stitch a machine seam along the tacked line, leaving a gap of about 2ft (60cm) in the centre of one side. Either side of the gap, go over the seam several times with machine stitching to strengthen it. While you are stitching this seam, work with the stained glass section on top so that you can ensure your stitching line is parallel to the other parts of the border.

**13** Clip the corners, trim the seams and turn the cushion cover right side out: press.

**14** Fold the raw edges on the opening in towards the centre and press. Tack the zip between them so that the folded edges meet in the centre of the zip, and stitch down each side by hand or machine; add extra stitches at the bottom of the zip as you stitch to strengthen it.

**15** Put the two pieces of calico right sides together and stitch a seam half an inch (1cm) round each edge, leaving about 12in (30cm) open for filling. Clip the corners and trim the seams, then turn the shape right side out and press. Fold the raw edges of the opening towards the middle and press.

**16** Fill the cushion pad about two-thirds full with polystyrene beads or foam chippings, then pin the two folded edges together along the gap. Stitch the edges together by machine, and insert the cushion pad into the cushion. Zip up the opening, and your floor cushion is complete.

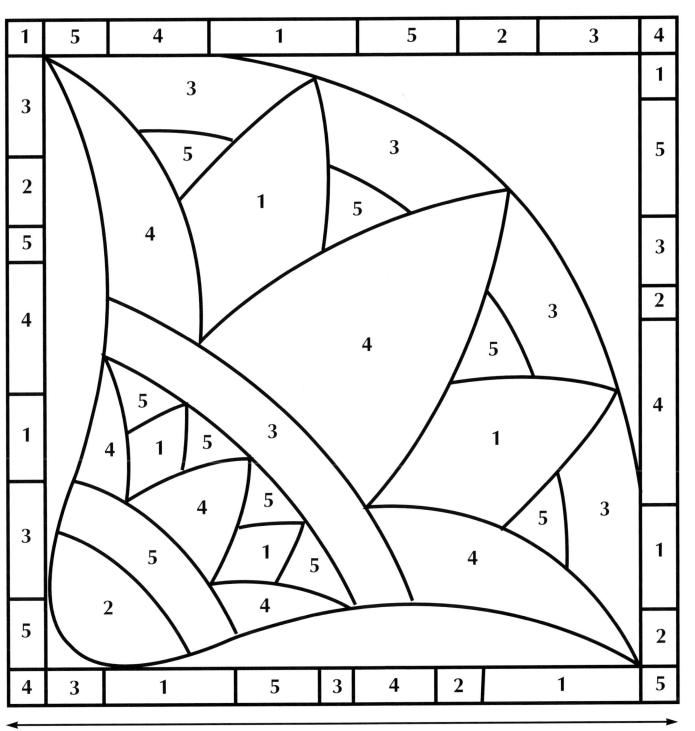

ENLARGE TO 48IN (122CM) SQUARE

## VARIATIONS

*If you're planning a different colour-scheme for this cushion, think bold! Try peach, green and cream with a maroon or dark forest green edging, or shades of autumnal colours such as rust, gold, tan and yellow bound in dark brown.*

**KEY**

*Areas without numbers are the background fabric*

1 Mid blue  2 Pale blue
3 Very pale blue  4 Blue print
5 Dark yellow

# PROJECT 15

# Waves Bed Quilt

*The grand finale project: a spectacular double bed quilt in a Chinese-inspired blue and white colourscheme. Despite its size, this design is really very straightforward to put together; the patches are large, and the curved lines are simple to bind. Each wave patch is created in a different fabric, blending from dark at the base to very pale and the top, and a touch of stylised foam is added to the tops of the waves in lace fabric.*

## PREPARATION

1   Enlarge the pattern on page 79 to the correct size; you will probably find it easiest to do this on several sheets of dressmakers' tracing paper, which comes in large sheets. Go over all the lines with black felt pen to make them stronger, and draw in all the numbers as marked.

2   Lay one piece of the very pale blue sheeting over the enlarged design, and trace all the solid lines with pencil. Mark the numbers in very lightly, in case they show through the paler patches.

## MAKING UP

3   Lay all your fabrics out so that they shade from dark to light. Your darkest fabric should go in section 1 marked on the design, and the lightest in section 18; depending on the fabrics you have chosen you should be able to put the others between them in numerical order, but feel free to adjust them within the pattern so that they look best. When you have decided which goes where, cut the enlarged pattern along the marked lines, section by section, to make templates; use these to cut patches out of the appropriate fabrics. Put all the pieces inside the marked design on the foundation piece, assembling them like a jigsaw puzzle, and tack them in position.

4   Now use the parts of the template marked 19 and 20 to cut patches out of the lace fabric; tack these in position on the background sheeting.

5   Use the opalescent fabric paint to add some spray drops above the waves; make them teardrop-shaped, with the point of the drop towards the wave, and paint them in a variety of sizes with the largest nearest the waves. When the paint is completely dry, fix it according to the manufacturer's instructions.

## MATERIALS

- Two pieces of very pale blue sheeting, 72 x 78in (1.8m x 2m)
- One piece of 2oz wadding, 72 x 78in (1.8m x 2m)
- Half a yard/metre of 18 different cotton fabrics, plains and prints, in different shades of blue
- Half a yard/metre of white lace fabric – I used net curtain fabric!
- Half a yard/metre of plain white fabric
- About 25yd/25m Coats cotton bias binding in white, 3/4in (2cm) wide when folded
- About 10yd/10m Coats cotton bias binding in dark or mid blue, 3/4in (2cm) wide when folded
- Sylko or Drima sewing thread in white and dark blue
- One skein of thick silver thread or fine silver cord
- White quilting thread
- Large and small sewing needles
- Opalescent and blue glitter fabric paints
- Soft pencil
- Paper, pencil, black felt pen, dressmakers' tracing paper etc for enlarging the pattern

6 Now begin adding and stitching the bias binding outlines, pressing the curves with a steam iron to set them. Begin by tacking and stitching the lines above and underneath the top wave; at the tips of the lacy sections, fold the binding to make neat points. Work your way down the quilt to the bottom: as you add lines, they will seal in the raw edges of the lines above them.

7 Stitch a few wave-like lines across the lacy sections that make up the wave-tops: you can do this by hand or machine. Lace is more liable than ordinary fabric to get caught on things, and these lines of stitching help to secure it to the backing.

8 Enlarge the fish designs on page 80 to the correct size, and use them to trace five fish shapes onto the piece of white fabric. Cut five body shapes from some of the excess blue and white fabrics, and pin each body onto a fish; for each fish then cut two fin shapes from a different blue and white fabric. Tack these into position.

9 Paint in the eye shapes with a little blue glitter paint; when it is completely dry, set it according to the manufacturer's instructions. Tack the fish in your chosen positions on the quilt, then stitch round all the lines of each fish shape with medium-width machine satin stitch in white.

## FINISHING

10 Press the second piece of pale blue sheeting and lay it out on a flat surface; position the wadding on top. On top of the wadding lay the stained glass design, right side up, and make a grid of horizontal and vertical lines of tacking across the quilt to secure the three layers together.

11 Using the silver thread or fine silver cord, work a line of quilting through all the layers using large running stitches. This quilting is quite bold rather than subtle! Use the dotted lines on the design opposite to give you a rough guide where to stitch, but you don't need to stick slavishly to this: you could use more or fewer lines.

12 Now use white thread to quilt round the water splashes at the tops of the waves. You can add a line of quilting round each fish, too, if you wish.

13 Fold the quilt in half down the centre line so that the bottom left and bottom right portions are face to face. Check that the curves are even on the bottom corners: if not, trim them to the same shape using sharp scissors so that they don't distort.

14 Finally, add the outer binding. Cut a strip of the blue bias binding to fit the top edge of the quilt, unfold it, and lay it face down along the front top, raw edges aligned. Stitch along the fold line, turn it over to the back, fold under the raw edge and stitch it in place by hand or machine. Bind round the rest of the quilt with one strip, turning under the raw ends at the top and securing them.

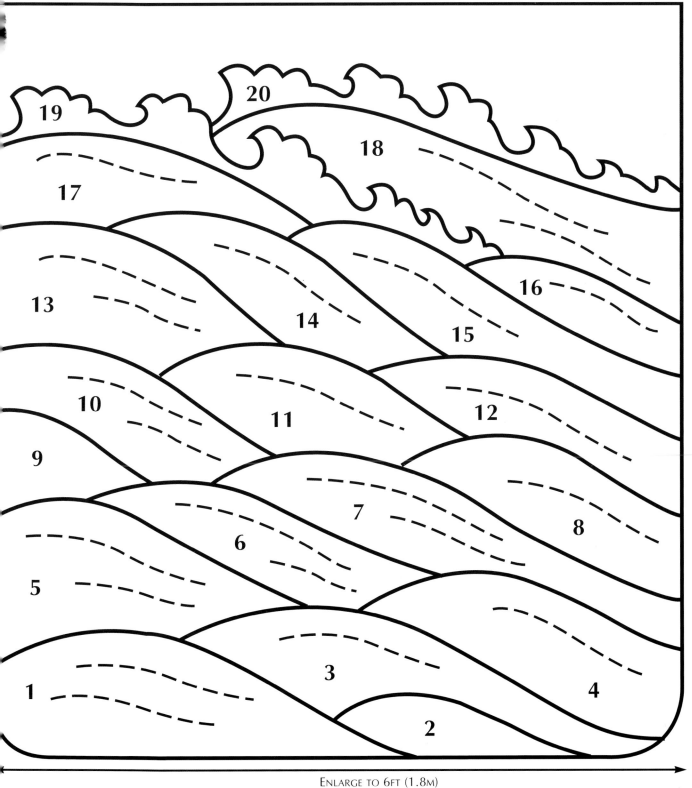

ENLARGE TO 6FT (1.8M)

**STITCHING SEQUENCE:**

**A** Begin by adding the binding along the top and bottom edges of the upper line of foam (piece 20); pleat the binding neatly to make sharp points at the tops of the waves.

**B** Now add the binding round the top edge of the lower line of foam (piece 19).

**C** Do the tops of waves 17 and 16, then add all the lines above the other waves in descending order.

PROJECT 15: WAVES BED QUILT

ENLARGE TO 10IN (25CM)

PROJECT 15: WAVES BED QUILT